TABLE OF CONTENTS

CASE STUDIES EPISODES

ABSTRACT

Massive change on a global scale, driven by the subscription economy and cloud-enabled technology, are making (and breaking) traditional business models at an alarming rate. However, change also generates excellent opportunities for agile organizations properly positioned to adapt.

To address these disruptive changes, a wide variety of B2B solutions are being introduced at an astonishing pace across all industry segments — leading to significant challenges for both buyers and sellers of these solutions. Buyers are challenged with the 'what-to-invest-in' decision and expect sellers to help (a) quantify the value of their solutions in a transparent way and (b) measure value realized post solution implementation. Sellers seek a credible way to respond, while differentiating their solutions from competitive alternatives. However, studies show that as many as 60% of buying opportunities end with a 'No Decision' outcome due to a lack of compelling content to overcome the inertia of maintaining the status quo.

*To bridge this buyer-seller 'expectations gap,' this book makes the point that **all buyer-seller interactions need to be based on business value**. As a consequence, the role of the Value Practitioner continues to evolve and grow increasingly important. The book focuses on **WHAT** this role is, **WHY** it is important, and **HOW** it bridges the gap. In short, it provides insights and best practices that will help establish the required agile Customer Value Management (CVM) environment and unleash the power of the Value Practitioner as a key player.*

PREFACE

"Agility is the ability to adapt and respond to Change... agile organizations view change as an opportunity, not a threat."

Jim Highsmith

"Everyone thinks of changing the world, but no one thinks of changing himself."

Leo Tolstoy

Motivation: Two Perspectives on WHY this book

John Porter and I spent much of business careers in the enterprise B2B software market place — working with a range of businesses from early stage start-ups to multi-billion corporations. We have both worked on the buyer and seller side of the business equation.

While much has been said (and written) on the importance of business value selling, we both were perplexed by how little has been done to institutionalize best practices. So, we decided to collaborate on this book to share our experiences and knowledge with you.

This book provides our perspective on the current state and future of the Customer Value Management (CVM) discipline. It's intended for Value Practitioners — those currently in the role or those considering it.

It gets into What's changed and How the need for an agile customer value management environment is opening the door for a more expansive career opportunity for Value Practitioners — balancing your contributions to the success of the business with a fulfilling quality of life.

In short, it's about what it takes to unleash customer value.

We begin by providing you with a bit of information on our background and perspectives.

Perspective One: John Porter, Chief Technology Officer, DecisionLink

Jim Berryhill and I started DecisionLink after many years experiencing the significant impact of selling based on business value. Specifically, we found that value selling resulted in consistently shorter sales cycles, higher average sale prices (ASP), and best in class close rates. However, we also observed that there was no technology to scale the delivery of value conversations across the entire sales cycle for the enterprise.

Consequently, DecisionLink was founded with the mission of bringing business value to every customer conversation through technology. To that end, we have spent the last decade working with enterprise class customers who shared this desire. The outcome: the creation of a customer value automation platform that standardizes how value is communicated anywhere in the customer lifecycle — ValueCloud™. In a nutshell, ValueCloud™ is a sales self-service, secure, software-enabled platform that supports the complete customer value life cycle.

As customers used and helped improve the platform, it also became apparent that this value automation technology required an educational component to drive consistent learnings and to share best practices in enabling an entire sales organization to change their sales approach. So, if you want to be a hero to your company and not just a hero on a deal, a repeatable and scalable way to facilitate value conversations is of paramount importance.

With the highly competitive global economy and the changing sales landscape, it is now more important than ever to support your opportunities with business cases to help your buyer get the funding for their initiative, and hence your products, solutions, and services. Moreover, your customers will be under increasing pressure to defend their initial investment decisions based on the business value achieved.

If your team is not equipped to support your buyers to do this, you are at a distinct disadvantage!

Perspective Two: Robert T. Caravella, Value Practice Leader

I had the opportunity to experience and witness the life and times of the Value Practitioner in a number of capacities over a 20-year period. First, I was a 'Lone Ranger,' building a Business Value Consulting (BVC) practice from ground zero for an *early stage* software company. Then I expanded the practice to manage a worldwide team of Value Practitioners. And finally, I was the head of a Value Engineering Center of Excellence for a *mature* $3.5 billion software business unit. Oh, and we integrated the business value models of a dozen acquired B2B software companies along the way.[1]

Through this experience, I witnessed first-hand the evolution of the Value Practitioner as I sought to bridge the buyer-seller value experience gap. In a nutshell, here are the seller-side challenges I ran into:

1. **Too little**. There were never enough Practitioners to satisfy the demand for business case support. Only about 10% of deals were supported by a rigorous business case.

2. **Too late**. Value Practitioners were called in for deals that were 'in trouble' — usually because the Economic Buyer wasn't seeing the solution value.

3. **Not Enough and Too Much**. Relevant, reusable content required to engage decision makers was simply not available. Every deal required customized content (spreadsheets, PPT, Word documents)
   to accommodate variations in company size, industry, geography, and use cases.

4. **Too Many**. Every business case exercise is an iterative process involving multiple players. Every change affected every output - a laborious process that led to frustration and errors.

5. **Leaving the Door Open**. Lastly, once a deal was closed, there was no way to measure value realized. This provided an opening for competitors.

Perhaps worse, the buyers were also frustrated. While they expected and needed vendor support, they were skeptical about the results of overly-simplistic vendor ROI calculators and lack of business case

---

[1] At one point, I managed a team of Business Value Consultants responsible for supporting a worldwide field organization of over 1000 sales and sales engineers, while managing a back-office group of ROI modelers responsible for building and maintaining a library of over 30 B2B solutions, developing courseware, reusable proposal content, and delivering enablement training.

transparency. They did not have time to listen to product pitches from sales reps who failed to talk credibly about the business value of solving their problems. And without evidence of value realized for their current investments, they could not justify expanding implementation to other parts of the business.

Since those hectic line management days, I have also had the opportunity to consult with companies across a variety of industries and solution domains to help establish more effective Customer Value Management practices. Surprisingly, many sellers and buyers continue to face these same issues and challenges today. And given the rate of change, where technology is making and breaking business models at an astonishing pace, the need for a more agile approach to customer value management has never been greater.

Audience: WHO Should Read This?

This book is intended for Value Practitioners seeking to gain further best practice insights from their peers, or for individuals trying to understand what the role entails as a career and professional growth opportunity.

The Value Practitioner role is critical to achieving higher close rates, increased average deal size, improved customer retention, and increased account growth through cross-sell and up-sell. To begin, it's important to understand that the role of Value Practitioner[2] is referred to in a variety of ways by different organizations — Business Value Consultant, Value Expert, Value Engineer, Value Analyst, Cloud Economist, to name a few.

Regardless of label, there are a number of Value Practitioner career opportunities for you to consider that depend on your personal goals and strengths. Generally speaking, these opportunities fit into two broad categories: (1) field-facing activities and (2) back office support, outlined as follows.

---

[2] We will refer to the role as 'Value Practitioner' throughout this document

1. **'Field-facing'** Value Practitioners work directly with the field sales teams to engage <u>prospects</u> and <u>existing customers</u> in value conversations throughout the engagement process — leading to (a) a business case that justifies investing in a B2B solution and (b) an assessment of value realized post implementation. Individuals that enjoy customer contact and working on the front lines to help close specific opportunities typically follow this career path.

2. **'Back-office'** support is essential to achieve the goals of scalability, repeatability, and consistency of high-quality deliverables. This role involves largely, but not exclusively, working behind the scenes with your internal stakeholders (sales, sales operations / enablement, marketing, product management, and customer care organizations) to create and maintain <u>reusable content</u> that the field sales teams need to engage prospects and customers. This content typically includes: value models, customer ROI case studies, proposal boilerplate, deal success stories, and enablement training courseware. To achieve this goal, two key processes must be formalized: (1) an <u>internal</u> collaboration process for understanding the expectations and 'demand' of your stakeholders and (2) an <u>external</u> customer engagement process that clarifies how and when to use sales assets and collateral. Success in this role requires aligning content with your go-to-market strategy and supporting your organization's prescribed selling approach (e.g., Challenger, MEDDIC, Miller Heiman, etc.).

Whether you are new to the role or experienced in the use of value engineering tools (Excel or commercial off-the-shelf products), this book provides insights and best practices that should be helpful.

CVM Benefits to You: WHY read it

The purpose of this book is to share best practices knowledge with you. It provides insights, reusable frameworks, and lessons learned from value experts who have blazed the trail over the past 20 years.

We settled on the tag line 'Unleashing Customer Value' to emphasize the opportunity for Value Practitioners to take on a more expansive, strategic role as an agent for the transformation to an agile customer value management world. We understand that this requires thinking outside the traditional box, but the potential benefits to you and the business are worthy of consideration.

- **Become a strategic player**. Establishing an agile CVM Program is a transformative change for your enterprise – leading to competitive differentiation and more profitable revenue growth. These goals are achieved in two ways. First, agile CVM reinforces your credibility as a **Trusted Advisor** for each opportunity you work on because you are uniquely positioned to bridge the gap between buyer and seller expectations. Second, and perhaps more importantly, an agile CVM Program is completely **scalable.** Now, in addition to being a hero for a given opportunity you can be a hero to your entire organization.

- **Grow professionally**. The framework and practices described in this book will help you add significant value to the sales, marketing, product management, and customer success business functions — often in a unique way. Because the role of Value Practitioner requires a great deal of first-hand customer interaction, you will also gain valuable experience across a number of industries.

Acknowledgements

We would like to thank the people who helped us in so many ways with this project.

First and foremost, we thank Jim Berryhill, DecisionLink CEO, for his support and encouragement throughout this endeavor. John and I have known and worked with Jim in a variety of capacities over the past two plus decades. In a sense, 'we have all grown up together' witnessing the transformation from technical product selling to differentiated business value selling as described in this book. As a senior sales executive for decades, Jim fully appreciates the organizational and technology challenges associated with this transformation. It was his vision, skill, and perseverance to build a business to do something about it.

We would also like to thank other members of the DecisionLink team for their support, valuable insights, and candid feedback.

- Gabe Vidal, VP Implementation Services
- Cliff Elam, SVP Product Strategy
- Josh Lankford, Senior Director Customer Value Management
- Kristina Cutter, Senior Director of Customer Enablement
- Andrew Abdalla, Customer Value Management Director
- Deanna Spinelli, Associate Value Engineer
- Lizzie O'Rourke, Director of Marketing
- June Price, Creative Director

Finally, we wish to thank Joanne Moretti, CEO JCurve Digital Partners LLC, for providing a Chief Marketing Officer perspective that is built into the case study. Tips from her white paper 'The Value Practitioner's Guide to Branding your Value Management Program for the Ultimate Impact' are incorporated in Episode 1 of the case study herein.

PART 1
THE CASE FOR ACTION:
WHY CHANGE? WHY NOW?

Part 1. The Case for Action: Why Change? Why Now?

"Change is the law of life and those who look only to the past or present are certain to miss the future." John F. Kennedy

Setting the Stage with a Real-world Case Study

To provide a practical backdrop for the narrative in this book, we use a case study — a composite of actual real-world events that occurred across a number of companies in different industries and B2B solutions (e.g., cybersecurity, IT Service Management, DevSecOps, etc.). While the details are fictionalized, all the stories (treated as 'Episodes') are true. They actually happened — including the quotes from the actors. Here's the story line to set the stage for what follows in this book.

CyberSecure Company (CSC) is the seller. As an early stage business, CSC has aggressive growth plans — seeking to become a dominant player in the Cloud Transformation security market space and positioning itself for an IPO within 3-5 years. It plans to do this by growing revenue profitably — adding new customers and expanding its footprint in existing accounts. The key protagonists are Peter Sellers (Sales Account Executive), Susan Smart (Value Practitioner), and John Cash (Chief Revenue Officer).

Susan has a solid reputation in CSC. She has built and successfully used an Excel-based value calculator to help close a number of large deals in the US. However, she is essentially a 'lone ranger' and demand for her support is growing. She does not have the bandwidth to support the entire sales channel. Consequently, Susan sees a number of challenges on the horizon:

- CSC is growing rapidly, adding new sales reps in the Americas, Europe, and Asia-Pacific.

- She is often called in late in the sales cycle for deals that are 'in trouble' — usually because solution value was not positioned early enough to capture the attention of the Economic Buyer.

- The model she uses requires a great deal of customization for each opportunity to account for different sales scenarios — (customer size, industry, solution use cases, and geography) — leading to a large collection of model variations that need to be maintained.

- Building a business case for a specific deal is an iterative approach. Each iteration leads to revised content that needs to be copied and pasted from her spreadsheets into appropriate customer-facing presentations — taking hours of time.

- Lastly, customers are now asking for a way to measure value realized relative to the baseline business case model. Currently, she has no credible way to do this — opening the door for competitors to enter the picture, jeopardizing renewals, and raising obstacles to account expansion.

A new CRO, John Cash, has just been hired to drive aggressive revenue growth. John recognizes the need for a sales transformation program — from technical product selling to a value selling model. Susan sees this as the opportunity she's been waiting for — to propose a more comprehensive Customer Value Management (CVM) program for the company.

ABC Financial Services is the buyer. ABC offers a broad range of services to consumers and small businesses like checking accounts, savings accounts, investments, as well as credit and loans for homes, cars, personal and business needs. Given the nature of the business, the security and privacy of their customer data is paramount. The key players are Harry Ross, Chief Information Officer and Mildred Pierce, Chief Security Officer (CSO). Harry is alarmed by the results of a security audit. He asks Mildred Pierce to respond with a proposal and plan.

The story unfolds as a series of 'episodes' in parallel with the best practices narrative in each part of the book. Other 'actors' in this narrative are introduced below.

Figure1.1: Meet the Actors in the CVM Case Study

CyberSecure Company (CS)	ABC Financial Services Company (Buyer Personas)
• Susan Smart, Value Practitioner. A talented Business Value Consultant who created the original CyberSecure value model in excel and recognizes the need for a more comprehensive approach to ensure enterprise-wide scalability • Peter Sellers, Sales Account Executive. A seasoned sales rep who has ABC Financial Services as a target opportunity • John Cash, Chief Revenue Officer. Introducing a sales transformation program — from technical product selling to a value selling model • Justin Tyme, CEO and founder. An industry expert in cybersecurity for virtualized data centers and public and private clouds. • Lauren Profit, CFO. Came up through the financial ranks; instrumental in helping CyberSecure raise $50M in Series C funding. • Vincent Price, CMO. Recognizes that an account-based marketing program will drive more quality leads.	Harry Ross, Chief Information Officer (CIO) Mildred Pierce, Chief Security Officer (CSO)

Before we get into the life and times of these actors, let's take a step back and characterize the current state of B2B buyer-seller expectations and introduce the key frameworks that will be used throughout this book.

****

The Challenging Business Landscape: Buyer and CSO Expectations are Higher than Ever

It's no secret that businesses today face great challenges from global competition, mergers and acquisitions, technology advancements, digital transformation, rising consumer expectations, and cybersecurity threats. The need for cost-effective B2B solutions to deal with these challenges has never been greater. As a result, horizontal and vertical competitive B2B solutions continuously enter the marketplace at an astonishing pace, leaving buyers with the tough decisions: 'Why Buy? Why Now? Why from a specific provider?' Imagine yourself an enterprise buyer trying to prioritize and purchase among the solutions listed in Figure 1.2. Daunting!

However, in a seemingly paradoxical convergence of interests, buyer and seller expectations are precisely the same when it comes to justifying investments in these B2B solutions. Both parties recognize that their key to success is an effective business case to justify investments and the ability to measure and showcase business value after the solution is implemented.

Moreover, Figure 1.2 has another important implication. It suggests that a typical enterprise has a long list of potential projects to fund. So, buyers and sellers need a credible way to 'rack and stack' investment priorities. After all, it's not just a question of convincing decision makers that your problem is worth solving. It's a question of 'hurdling' other projects in the queue and moving up the funding priority list.

In fact, industry analyst research reports that 90% of buyers require quantifiable evidence of business benefits before investing. Yet two-thirds of buyers confess that they are poorly equipped with knowledge and tools to create a credible business case, while over four-fifths of buyers look to their suppliers for assistance in quantifying value.[2]

---

[2] IDC Customer Experience Survey and Customer Experience Panel.

Figure 1.2: Proliferation of B2B Solutions: Tough Choices for Buyers; Competitive Differentiation Challenges for Sellers

SOLUTION	PROBLEM DESCRIPTION
Cloud / Cyber-security	Protect against the criminal or unauthorized use of electronic data and resources.
IT Service Management (ITSM)	Deal with the implementation and management of quality IT services — typically, IT service providers (internal IT or MSPs).
IT Asset Management (ITAM)	Manage and optimize the purchase, deployment, maintenance, use, and disposal of software and hardware.
Human Capital Management (HCM)	Manage and maintain the workforce — human resource management systems (HRMS or HRIS)
Remote Monitoring of Assets (IoT)	Enable straightforward provisioning, management, and automation of connected devices within the Internet of Things
Project and Portfolio Management	Help project managers and organizations execute projects: unique initiatives with a set scope, timeline, and budget.
Customer Relationship Management (CRM)	Manage and analyze customer interactions and data throughout the customer lifecycle.
Marketing Automation	Help marketing departments market on multiple channels online (such as email, social media, etc.) and automate tasks.
Incentive Compensation Management (ICM)	Design and manage sales compensation plans — providing tools to improve employee ability to sell products or services.
Learning Management Systems (LMS)	Plan, implement, deliver and assess a specific learning process and assess student performance.
Talent Management Systems (TMS)	Address the "four pillars" of talent management: recruitment; performance, development; and compensation.
Enterprise Resource Planning (ERP)	Manage the business and automate many back-office functions related to technology, services and human resources.
Hospitality Management	Manage hotel properties and associated services to ensure the best experience to for guests.
Customer Value Management (CVM)	Help (a) marketing with generating more qualified leads through account-based marketing programs; (b) sales teams with assets to carry on meaningful value conversations throughout the customer engagement cycle; and (c) customer success teams measure and showcase value realized post B2B solution implementation
Mobile Management	Administration of mobile devices, such as smartphones, tablet computers and laptops.
Digital Content Management (DCM)	Support the collection, management, and publishing of information stored and accessed via computers.
Server and Desktop Virtualization	Create of a virtual computer environment — delivered to a user in place of a physical computer.
Application Management	Manage the application life cycle – from design, testing and improvement of applications that are part of IT services.
Healthcare	Electronic medical records (EMR), health information exchanges, medical care support systems.
Telecom	Call center management, network administration, performance, availability, security, regulatory compliance
Retail	Data management, reporting and business intelligence analytics, on-shelf availability, and point of sale applications

On the seller side, CSOs and CMOs understand that quantifying and selling the business value of their solutions is critical to their success. After all, if only 10-15% of deals have a compelling business case, how much money is being left on the table? A lot!

Yet this awareness has not happened overnight. For those of us in the industry long enough, we've seen an evolution to the ultimate goal of Customer Value Management (CVM) as illustrated in the figure below.

Figure 1.3: The Evolution to Agile Customer Value Management (CVM) and Differentiated Value Selling

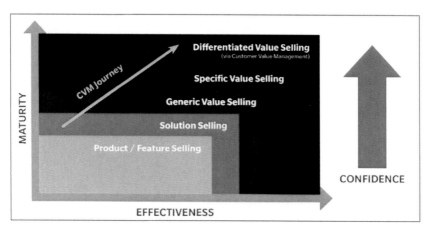

The evolution began with technical Product / Feature Selling decades ago — when there was a relatively straightforward way to map a product capability to a specific problem. As problems became more complex, buyers and sellers increasingly relied on Solution Selling to define and scope requirements and design more sophisticated solutions. As competition stiffened further, a Generic Value Selling model appeared — where sellers provided buyers with generic examples of the value achieved by other organizations. But these generalized value propositions were not specifically relevant to each organization; they did not always account for industry, geography, size, or use case variations. This led to Specific Value Selling methodologies that enabled value to be quantified and customized for each opportunity. Agile Customer Value Management completes this evolution. Specifically, CVM brings organizations to the level of Differentiated Value Selling — where value is quantified for a specific project including differentiation from other alternative uses of budget such as direct competition or alternative uses of capital.

Given this evolution and a common motivation to achieve the differentiated value selling level of maturity, why do B2B buyers report that only one-fifth of their sales representatives are genuinely interested in understanding their business challenges?[3] Why are buyers chagrined that four-fifths of sales representatives just "pitch product" without bringing any value to the table? Why are CSOs often disappointed in the return on their investments in Customer Relationship Management (CRM) software and other sales ecosystem tools? Why are a growing number of sellers not achieving quota?

The answer to these questions has a lot to do with a missing link — a way to bridge the gap between buyer and seller expectations. Increasingly, companies are finding that this bridge is a formalized program and process, called Customer Value Management (CVM).

The need for an effective CVM Program opens the 'opportunity door' for a more expansive organizational role for the Value Practitioner. Specifically, it brings us to what this book is all about — specifically, providing insight and best practices for current or aspiring Value Practitioners to play a leadership role in launching a CVM Program internally, driving a value-focused customer engagement model, and measuring and showcasing business value.

We begin by assessing the state of the buyer-seller world as it exists today and what a better future could (and should) look like.

---

[3] Buyers do in fact add that another 30% at least try to understand how their solution will help the client.

What Does a GREAT Buyer-Seller Experience Look Like?

As previously mentioned, buyers desire to engage in initiatives that will help them achieve their organizational and personal objectives — and sellers seek to help buyers buy. However, both parties often find it difficult to overcome the allure of the status quo. So, what does a great seller-buyer experience look like?

The seller experience should seek to achieve four goals: gain the attention and support of a Champion and Economic Buyer; establish credibility with the decision maker and influencers; build a defensible business case; and lock-in a longer-term relationship as a Trusted Advisor. These goals can be achieved by three key actions:

1. **Grab attention with a provocative Value Hypothesis**. Based on your account research, internal account team knowledge, and industry benchmarks, a Value Hypothesis provides the Economic Buyer and Champion with a 'directional sense' of your solution's business value. The objectives of a value hypothesis are to (a) pique the buyer's curiosity enough to continue a meaningful dialogue and (b) gain agreement to collaborate on refining the value hypothesis into a defensible business case. Consequently, the value hypothesis provides a strawman model to drive a business case working session.

2. **Build a credible, transparent business case**. The same methodology used to build the value hypothesis is used to engage the buyer's team with a non-intrusive process leading to defensible business case. The objectives of the business case modeling exercise should be to: (a) gain buyer team consensus on the metrics required by the Economic Buyer to justify investment; (b) provide complete traceability from the ROI and payback calculations down to individual pain point-value statements pairs that comprise the business case; (c) help quantify the cost of delay; and (d) move the seller solution up the investment priority stack.

3. **Lock in an on-going relationship as Trusted Advisor**. The final business case model also serves as the baseline for periodically measuring and showcasing value realized following solution implementation. This part of the seller experience is critical to locking in renewals and setting the stage for expanded implementation through cross-sell and up-sell opportunities.

This seller scenario also contributes to a great buyer experience. Specifically, the Economic Buyer and Champion leverage a proven, rigorous methodology to (a) justify budget and set funding priorities that supports their current decision-making process and (b) provide evidence that their current investments are achieving the original ROI expectations.

It's a win-win situation: the buyer gets the solutions needed to achieve their business objectives and the seller achieves recognition as a Trusted Advisor. Sounds straightforward. But there are some challenges that sellers and buyers must overcome to achieve this great experience. The figure below illustrates today's challenges from both a seller and buyer perspective.

Figure 1.4: *Today's Landscape: Challenges Inhibiting a Great Buyer-Seller Experience*

The illustration suggests that sellers and buyers appear to live in a parallel universe. To clarify their different perspectives, the table below suggests what goes on in the minds of a typical buyer and seller today.

Figure 1.5: The Parallel Universe of Buyer-Seller Perspectives

Seller Perspective	Buyer Perspective
Access. I can't gain the attention of the Economic Buyer & Champion. I need better content to carry on business value conversations with decision makers. As a result, it takes too long to 'hit my numbers.'	I have limited time to engage with sales people — especially conversations centered on product capability instead of business value. I rely on my other staff members for technical due diligence. I'm also skeptical about overly-simplistic calculators and lack of business case transparency. I need to see a credible, transparent methodology that leads to defensible results.
Stakeholder Consensus. The Economic Buyer requires multiple people to weigh in on each major investment opportunity. How can I orchestrate buy-in across a variety of decision influencers with different expectations and motivations?	I need to have my team's consensus on which tools to buy. I'm looking for solid commitment from management team members before investing.
High Discounts erode quota attainment. Without showing value, it becomes a pricing war. It's tough to win a war without ammunition. High discounts and the dreaded 'No Decision' outcome erode quota attainment.	Unless I'm presented with compelling, defensible business value, the only way I can get this investment approved is through heavy discounting.

Seller Perspective	Buyer Perspective
<u>Locking in renewals and growing account</u>. Renewals are at risk and I can't cross-sell upsell because I can't show the value of my customer's current investment. Customers need help in justifying renewals and expanding a solution's footprint. How do we measure and showcase value of current investments?	I need a credible way to measure and showcase value realized to help justify renewals and expand implementation. I cannot invest more until the value of my current investment is proved.

The bottom line for a GREAT buyer-seller relationship is that a transparent business case with agreed upon numbers will always get budget. It's this premise that sets the stage for why an agile Customer Value Management Program is important to the business and you.

Customer Value Management (CVM): <u>WHAT</u> Is It and <u>WHY</u> Do It?

At its core, Customer Value Management is an approach to managing all aspects of the 'value journey' — from initial contact with prospective buyers to on-going customer relationship management following solution implementation. This journey consists of three distinct *collaborative* stages:

1. **Value Discovery**. Both the buyer and seller need a reason to initiate a meaningful conversation. Buyers need a 'directional sense' of potential business value: *'given your understanding of our business challenges, what is the potential business value of your solution for my organization?'* To respond, sellers need an efficient way to (a) gain *unique insights* into the buyer's business needs; (b) *reach* the Economic Buyer and *frame* the conversation around potential business outcomes; and (c) *quantify* an 'outside-in' business *value hypothesis*. The goal: gain buyer agreement to collaborate on a business case to justify investing in seller's solution.

2. **Value Delivery.** This collaboration consists of first, determining the solution benefits that are relevant to the buyer and then, quantifying them according to the buyer's input. The goal: create a transparent business case, transfer ownership to the Economic Buyer, and implement the B2B solution successfully setting the stage for periodically quantifying value achieved.

3. **Value Realization**, following a successful implementation, measures actual *value achieved* relative to the original baseline ROI model — helping the customer *showcase business value*. This stage leads to a satisfied customer, helps lock-in renewals, and opens the door to cross-sell / upsell opportunities. In addition, customer testimonials and case studies along with benefit proof points should be captured and fed back into the value models for continued refinement and enrichment.

By achieving these goals, CVM complements and enhances the traditional Customer Relationship Management (CRM) discipline. Specifically, by adding insights and assets that enable value-centric conversations at each customer interaction touchpoint, CVM helps customers achieve success, which in turn accelerates seller success — a win-win value proposition for buyers and sellers.

CVM Benefits to the Business

Over the past few years, books have been written and significant research has been conducted on the benefits of selling business value.

- *The Challenger Sale* by Matthew Dixon and Brent Adamson, emphasizes that sales conversations must be *tailored* to align with each buyer's *economic value drivers.*

- Reed K. Holden in his book, *Negotiating with Backbone,* argues that the 'game' of selling is actually a test of sales rep *confidence* in solution price and value.

- Miller Heiman, in its *2018 CSO Insights Study*, reports some eye-opening statistics on the buyer-seller experience as shown in the table below.

Figure 1.6: Research Findings on the Business Benefits of CVM

Buyer experience	Seller experience
• Only **31.8%** of customers say their sales reps exceed expectations • Only **23%** of buyers look to "Vendor Salespeople" as a top-three resource to solve business problems. • **92%** of buyers want to hear a value proposition EARLY in sales cycle • Only **31.9%** of buyers feel there is significant differentiation from one vendor to the next • **70%** of customers have already defined needs and have decided to purchase something before they engage salespeople	• Only **53%** of sales reps achieved quota in 2017 down from 63% in 2011 • Sales leaders feel that only **50%** of their team members can do a proper needs analysis, and only **46%** of their team members can create an ROI/Cost-Benefit analysis • Only **7.5%** of Sales Leaders feel their team members have established themselves as Trusted Advisors with clients

More recently, IDC published a research report[4] noting that value-selling at a cloud-based software company led to a 70% improvement in close rates with net-new accounts, along with improved upselling close rates from approximately 70% to 75%. IDC's recipe for success includes producing scalable, sharable, and reusable models that can monitor value delivery post sale along with an automation platform that supports economic value analysis for every rep.

And in April 2020, Dimensional Research conducted a value management survey[5] of 203 qualified individuals working at B2B SaaS companies with more than 50 sales reps in a sales, sales

---

[4] IDC Perspective: *'Value Selling: The Only Way to Close in 2020,'* Gerry Murray
[5] For the survey, **value management** is defined as to the practice of systematically capturing, analyzing, measuring and communicating the economic value achieved to confirm the expected and actual business contributions of a relationship.

enablement, or value consultation leadership roles. The findings noted that 82% of customers ask for value tools beyond what these organizations are capable of providing. Not surprisingly, they also report that over 90% of sellers report that they struggle with value management.

It's important to realize that the significance of the above metrics to a business depends on where you are in stage of growth and business maturity. For example, *early stage enterprises* are most likely interested in value differentiation, to ensure profitable revenue growth. These enterprises measure success in terms of improved marketing campaign conversions, lead conversions to sales qualified deals, close rates, discount reduction, and deal velocity. While a *late stage business* may want to focus on protecting margins and renewals. Thus, achieving reduced customer churn, while increasing opportunities for cross-sell/up-sell are important performance metrics.

Regardless of stage, it's helpful to frame the benefits of your CVM program in terms of its value to the end-to-end marketing and sales processes:

**Marketing Campaign → Marketing Qualified Lead → Sales Qualified Opportunity →
Forecast → Close Deal → Customer Success**

We'll explore each of these processes in more detail later in the book. However, now that we understand **WHAT** CVM is about and **WHY** to do it, let's discuss **HOW** to make this kind of transformative change happen.

Making Change Happen: Advice from the Experts

"Success today requires the agility and drive to constantly rethink, reinvigorate, react, and reinvent." — Bill Gates

"Agility is the ability to adapt and respond to Change...agile organizations view change as an opportunity, not a threat."
— Jim Highsmith

Building an effective CVM Program requires driving change across three dimensions — people, process, and technology. While the right process, practices, and tools represent the 'infrastructure' underpinning of CVM, it's getting people to use this infrastructure that is critical to success. So how do you get people (customers and internal stakeholders) to jump into a better future with you? How do you transform an organizational culture and make it stick?

In the 20th Century, Edgar H. Schein (considered by many to be the father of the corporate culture field), introduced a seemingly straightforward, 3-step model for changing a corporate culture: (1) '**unfreeze**' the current culture; (2) '**transform**' it to a desired future state; and (3) '**refreeze**' the new culture." Sounds simple. But what does this really mean? And how can we embed this approach into our notion of a 'CVM journey?'

Figure 1.7: Edgar Schein's 3-Step Culture Change Model

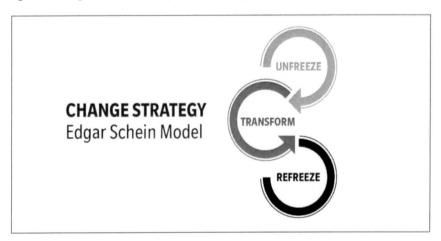

Let's elaborate on these concepts.

1. **'Unfreezing'** involves *raising awareness* and *motivating* people to want to change. It addresses the questions:" Why Change? Why Now? It requires getting key players in different business functions to recognize **WHY** change is critical to their business success. You need to paint a picture of a better future — one that is within everyone's best interests and grasp. You must also explain the risks of doing nothing.

2. **Transformation** is about implementing the changes required to move the organization steadily to the desired future state. It requires (a) a business case to justify investing in process, tools, and people and (b) creating an actionable plan that clarifies **WHAT** needs to be done to achieve a higher state of 'readiness' and **HOW** to do it.

3. **'Refreezing'** requires *reinforcing* behavior to reach a 'steady state' where this change is permanent. It requires implementing the right tools, measuring results, demonstrating success, and establishing practices that ensure *continuous process improvement*.

Achieving these goals requires a CVM Change Management Framework — one that clarifies the attributes associated with each step of Schein's change paradigm. As illustrated below, these attributes need to be taken into account at every stage of the CVM journey. Specifically:

1. Have we *motivated* all stakeholders to change to a 'better way' and created a bias for action?

2. Have we created the *know-how* in terms of knowledge and content to deliver on this promise?

3. Have we properly *enabled* stakeholders and certified their ability to perform at the desired level?

4. Do we have a program of continuous *reinforce*ment to lock in the transformation?

Figure 1.8: Using the Schein Model and CVM Change Management Frameworks to Clarify WHAT and HOW to Change

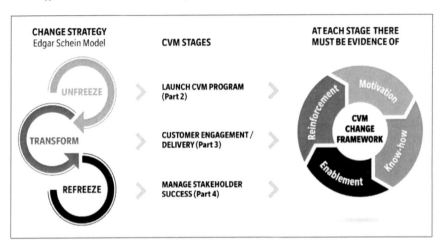

In this book, we use the Schein Model to provide the overarching structure for **WHAT** needs to be changed. Specifically, Part 2 (*Launching CVM*) focuses on 'unfreezing' the existing technical product selling culture. Part 3 (*CVM Delivery*) is all about executing the transformation to a differentiated value selling model. Part 4 (*Managing Customer Success*) addresses the requirement for 'refreezing' or locking in this new culture to achieve high performance results for both buyers and sellers. Within each Part, our CVM Change Management Framework provides the methodology to clarify **HOW** to make great things happen.

We begin by introducing a framework to embed this change model into the three key stages of the CVM Journey.

The Three Stages of the CVM Journey

As illustrated below, there are three distinct stages required to move an organization from a product selling to a solution value selling culture. For each stage, we note that our four change management attributes (Motivation, Know-how, Enablement, and Reinforcement) are central to the success of the surrounding activities.

Figure 1.9: The Three Stages of the CVM Journey

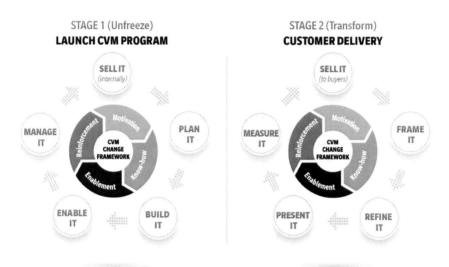

Stage 1: <u>Launch CVM (internally)</u>. In this first stage, we (1) sell the business value of a formal CVM program to senior management and build an internal network of advocacy, get buy-in to an actionable plan, and set expectations with a business case (*motivation*); (2) build the required content and establish the automation platform to engage prospective buyers and current customers (*know-how*); (3) *enable* all stakeholders through role-based training and on-the-job coaching; and (4) establish the processes to ensure adoption and continuous improvement of process and content (*reinforcement*).

Stage 2: <u>Customer Delivery (externally)</u>. Once the processes, content, infrastructure, and skill sets are in place, you're ready to engage buyers and customers. In this second stage, you (1) sell it to your Champion and Economic Buyer to get agreement to collaborate (*motivation*); (2) engage the buyer's team to select the specific benefits that comprise the business case (*know-how*); (3) build, refine, and present the resulting business case (*enablement*); and (5) gain agreement on the approach to measuring and showcasing value realized (*reinforcement*).

Stage 3: <u>Manage Customer Success</u>. Lastly, it's essential to lock-in your longer-term relationship as Trusted Advisor. In this 'steady state' stage, you must (1) perform periodic measurement of CVM adoption, usage, and effectiveness; (2) establish the cadence for periodically analyzing and presenting planned versus actual results; (3) promote success through customer-facing ROI Spotlights and internal deal success stories; and (4) refine the processes for continuous improvement.

In the pages that follow, we elaborate on the processes, practices, tools, and skills required to achieve success across these stages.

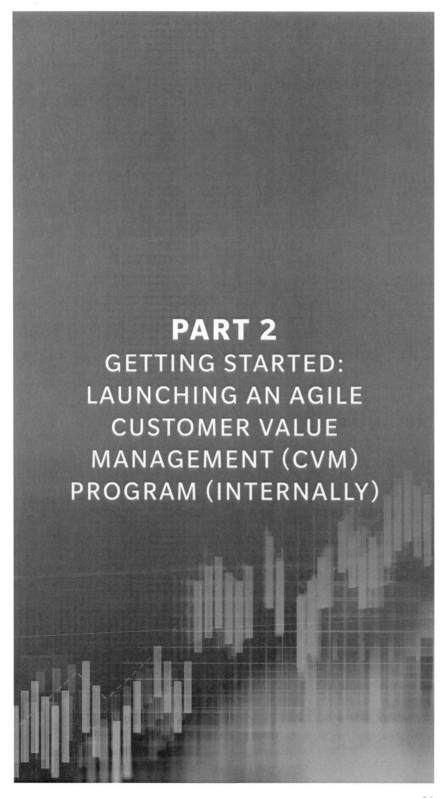

PART 2
GETTING STARTED:
LAUNCHING AN AGILE
CUSTOMER VALUE
MANAGEMENT (CVM)
PROGRAM (INTERNALLY)

Part 2. Getting Started: Launching an Agile Customer Value Management (CVM) Program (Internally)

"Leadership is about mobilizing a group of people to jump into a better future." —John P. Kotter, Matsushita Professor of Leadership, Emeritus, Harvard Business School

CVM Launch Goals:
'Unfreezing' a Product Selling Culture

To recap Part 1, launching an agile Customer Value Management (CVM) program is critical to the on-going success of your customers, your organization and your career. Accomplishing this goal requires 'unfreezing' an existing culture – *motivating* internal stakeholders to 'jump into a better future.' To make this happen, you need to provide stakeholders with the *know-how* to understand three things:

- Why Change?

- Why Now?

- Why CVM?

Figure 2.1: Motivating Stakeholders to Jump into a Better Future

WHY CHANGE?	WHY NOW?	WHY CVM?
• What specific business problem do we need to address? • Why this initiative?	• What is the compelling event? • What are the consequences of not acting swiftly?	• What are the specific benefits of CVM to each stakeholder? • How will stakeholder experience and behavior differ from the satus quo?

Key players in different business functions (typically sales, marketing, customer success, and finance) have to recognize **WHY** change is critical to their business success. So, you need to create a network of advocacy and a bias for action by painting a picture of a better future – one that is within everyone's interests and grasp.

CVM Launch Success Measures

To gain traction for a CVM Program, consider the following three critical success factors as evidence of a successful launch.

1. **Executive sponsorship**. Your CVM business case, implementation plan, and budget are approved. The business case should quantify the expected value in metrics that are meaningful and agreed to by the sponsoring executive (e.g., increased win rates; larger deal sizes; decreased churn; improved quota achievement, etc.).

2. **Stakeholder commitment**. You have a strong internal network of advocacy for the program. This requires understanding what each stakeholder stands to gain. Typically, the more buy-in you get from key stakeholders (e.g., Sales, Marketing, Product Management, Customer Success, Finance), the higher the likelihood of success.

3. **Customer validation** of CVM readiness to a go-live launch of the delivery program. You should conduct two or three pilots with 'friendly' customers. These pilots should provide evidence that (a) the process is non-intrusive and worth their investment in collaborating with you and (b) provides outputs that they agree add value (e.g., a transparent, defensible business case or an assessment that helps showcase value of their current investments).

Program Challenges

Achieving these outcomes requires recognizing and addressing a number of challenges.

Top-down Commitment. Transformation requires creating a top-down network of advocacy for a vision and actionable strategy. Early on, expectations of the impact of this transformation on work activities and behavior needs to be set, measurement and monitoring capabilities established, and accountability for adopting the new processes and technology clarified. Along the way, you may have to address the false perception that selling business value is a long drawn out process — that it delays the sales cycle rather than accelerates it. However, as one savvy sales executive notes, this is a myth.

"There is a common misperception that ROI lengthens the sales cycle. This is wrong; it will shorten it. In fact, the earlier we do it, the better. If you wait until a customer asks for it, you are too late."

Inertia caused by existing processes and tools. Many organizations have fragmented customer engagement processes and homegrown tools that require ROI gurus to use — inhibiting scalability, repeatability, adaptability, and consistency. It's likely that you will find a variety of Excel-based approaches that individuals are comfortable using, and reluctant to give up. Moreover, the absence of a consistent approach may lead to the perception that value messaging is for the "accountants," exacerbating sales team apprehension and reluctance.

Inconsistent, poor quality content that does not address the specific needs of different buyer personas. Not surprisingly, these fragmented processes and homegrown tools lead to issues in the quality of deliverables — often resulting in overly complex materials that make it difficult for sales teams to clearly explain how solution value is quantified. In addition, these traditional approaches are error-prone — leading to calculation and content errors that impeach credibility with the customer. It's no wonder that sales teams may be reluctant to adopt these approaches and when they do use them, find it difficult to gain customer buy-in to collaborate on a business case. Moreover, "one-size-fits-all" value models do not adequately respond to the nuances of a given engagement (e.g., industry, use case, or geographical variations) — leading to results that lack accuracy, impugn credibility, and feed the perception that value discussions may actually slow down a sales cycle.

Multiple Knowledge and Skill Variations to support. The A team players 'get it'; in fact, they are probably already value selling. The challenge is getting the B team players on board. How do you motivate *everyone* on the team to embrace a value-selling mindset? What tools, assets, and training are required to make this happen?

Continuous Improvement. Business change is constant and unrelenting. As a consequence, new products or enhancements to existing solutions are continuously introduced. Mergers and acquisitions also drive major changes. The CVM Program must continuously adapt to these changes. Mechanisms for handling feedback from buyers and customers to enhance the value models and associated assets are critical to success.

Guiding Principles and Framework for Successful CVM Start-up

To address these challenges and create an actionable program plan, it is helpful to have a framework in mind that properly integrates the process, technology, and people considerations of CVM together in a holistic way.

The illustration below provides an example of a framework and systematic approach to help you think through and launch a CVM Program internally. There are five key stages:

1. **SELL IT** addresses the need to *motivate* stakeholders — communicating a vision for a better future, gaining executive sponsorship, building a network of advocacy and the incentive to act now.

2. **PLAN IT** involves building the business case and plan to justify funding and resource commitment.

3. **BUILD IT** focuses on _know-how_ — establishing the required processes, acquiring tools, creating the content required to deliver and sustain the program; and ensuring customer validation before full 'go-live' rollout of the program begins.

4. **ENABLE IT** addresses the need to train stakeholders and promote adoption and usage of CVM assets.

5. **MANAGE IT** is all about _reinforcement_ — establishing the steady state processes to ensure continuous improvement.

Figure 2.2: Framework for Launching a CVM Program

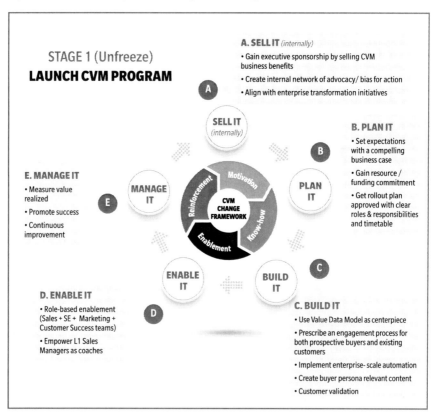

In the pages that follow, we drill down to explore the practices associated with each stage.

SELL IT – Best Practices to Create a Bias for Action

Do your Homework: Understand Stakeholder Expectations

CVM offers significant business benefits to stakeholders across the organization — sales, marketing, product management, and customer success. The Chief Revenue Officer (CRO), as a typical executive sponsor, will likely want to enlist their support for the program. Hence the leaders of these organizations should be part of your network of advocacy. So, you need to know who these stakeholders are, how CVM will help achieve their performance goals, and properly set expectations. The figure below suggests that there are a number of players who have a stake in CVM business outcomes, along with your key responsibilities.

Figure 2.3: CVM Program Stakeholders

Stakeholder	Value Practitioner Responsibilities
Executive Management	• Sell the program / gain sponsorship • Agree on success measures and reporting for adoption / usage of CVM process and assets
Sales Management	• Align CVM Program with sales process • Sell the program internally (how do I get the program off the ground?) • Ensure adoption post CVM rollout
Sales Reps	• Provide on-going business case support for opportunities
Sales Engineers	• Synchronize Proof of Value (POV) with business case value statements • Collect POV empirical data to support business case
Sales Enablement	• Develop CVM enablement training content • Support training delivery
Marketing	• Align Value Model with go-to-market strategy • Provide targeted account-based marketing content • Create customer ROI case studies
Product Management	• Maintain / enhance Value Model to reflect product changes • Suggest value-based enhancements to product line based on customer value engagements

Stakeholder	Value Practitioner Responsibilities
Customer Success	• Establish ROI Baseline and conduct Value Realization Assessments
Professional Services	• Establish ROI Baseline against which implementation success can be measured
Partners	• Support channel partners
Buyers + Customers	• New buyers. Engage prospective buyers to create defensible business case • Existing customers. Conduct periodic Value Realization assessments

This table suggests that the goals of the CVM Program need to be aligned with the expected business outcomes of *internal* business stakeholders, *external* partners, prospective buyers, and existing customers. Thus, to begin, it's important to understand the processes that each stakeholder owns and how they are measured.

By way of example, consider the key performance measures for sales management (executives and first line managers). The figure below suggests the processes and metrics that drive their behavior and hence what a CVM Program needs to address.

Figure 2.4: Sales Management Metrics that CVM Supports

Sales Process	Metrics that CVM Program Should Support
Campaign to Lead	✔ Increase marketing campaign response rates and Marketing Qualified Leads (MQLs) generated
Lead to Opportunity	✔ Higher conversion rate of MQLs to real opportunities, frequently referred to as Sales Qualified Leads (SQLs) ✔ Reduce time and effort associated with unqualified leads
Opportunity to Forecast	✔ Improve conversion rate of opportunities to forecast ✔ Reduce time and effort associated with Proof of Value / Proof of Concept ✔ Decrease Cost per Sale
Forecast to Close	✔ Increase Percentage Close Rate ✔ Increase Average Deal Size; Reduce Average Discount ✔ Increase Deal Velocity
After-sale / Customer Success	✔ Improve Retention rate; Reduce churn ✔ Increase Cross-sell/up-sell

You should perform this type of analysis for all stakeholders that you want to enlist in your network of advocacy, as it will help ensure that the CVM Program provides the required content and training for each group.

Build an Internal Network of Advocacy

Gaining buy-in and commitment for a CVM Program requires engaging key stakeholders to 'jump into a better future.' This requires creating a network of advocacy for a compelling vision (what will a better future look like for each stakeholder community) and building the business case to justify the required resources and investments.

CASE STUDY EPISODE 1: Communicating a Compelling Vision for a 'CyberValue Program'

To underscore the above principles, we begin with the opening act of the CyberSecure Case Study introduced in Part 1.

Recall that Susan Smart, CyberSecure Value Practitioner, recognized that selling the need for the CVM Program required getting John Cash, Chief Revenue Officer, on board as the executive sponsor. Over a relaxing lunch, Susan makes her case, resulting in an 'Agreement in Principle' from John to sponsor a CVM initiative.

However, John recognizes the need to get other players on board from Sales, Sales Engineering, Sales Operations, Marketing, and Customer Success. He also feels that giving the CVM program a **'brand name'** will help communicate and reinforce his message. John has a solid relationship with Vincent Price, CMO. He decides to ask Vincent for some advice on branding. After filling Vincent in on the goals and focus of the CVM Program, their conversation proceeds as follows.

John: So, what do you think of the idea Vincent. Do you see benefits to the marketing team?

Vincent: I most certainly do see how this kind of program could help us capture first-hand ROI data from customer experience. I can also see how downstream we could use it for account-based marketing. Sounds like you and Susan have already done the preliminary due diligence and have a vision and mission in mind. But I do agree that, even if you have the best idea in the world, if you don't market it properly, it will fail. So, I think branding your CVM Program will definitely help get it off the ground and help with its rollout. Here's my advice:

- First, keep in mind that in its simplest form a brand is a promise. The more you make and keep that promise, the more equity you transfer into your brand. Just as we make a promise to CyberSecure customers to provide enterprise class cybersecurity, you can drive your internal CVM initiative and mission by making a promise and keeping it.

- To begin, make sure that you "clarify and connect" the value the CVM initiative to our CyberSecure business strategies and goals. The three internal connection points should run along 3 vectors: 1) up and into our corporate goals, 2) laterally across into your peer's goals (including me!), and 3) down and outward into your sales team members' goals and aspirations. When goals are clearly shared in all three directions in terms that relate to their success, you will unify and lead through and with a common sense of purpose.

- Do not assume that communicating your Vision, Mission and Plan to one person at any one of those three levels I just described is enough. Repeat your story, over and over until you have really penetrated the company. Even if it seems repetitive to you, most people haven't heard it, and are too busy in their own day-to-day tasks to listen or understand what you are doing. Build a "deck" and take your pitch on the road.

- Demonstrate your alignment with corporate goals. Make sure that our CEO (Justin Tyme) and CFO (Lauren Profit) are on board with the program. From our last board meeting, we know that revenue growth, expanding our market share, and positioning for an IPO in a few years is key to their success. Connect the dots between CVM and these goals.

- Design your Brand name and style in accordance with our internal branding guidelines. I can help you with that. We just need 1 or 2 words that really communicate what you are promising. We want the name to resonate with both our internal stakeholders as well as our customers. How about 'CyberValue?' This label can be interpreted by our internal folks as meaning how we quantify and sell the value of CyberSecure solutions to buyers. On the flip side, buyers and customers can interpret it as helping them quantify value to justify the investments they need to protect their companies from cyberthreats.

- Lastly, constantly demonstrate and talk about your outcomes. At every opportunity you have, once you have communicated your plan to your subordinates, peers, or executives, make sure you always come prepared to share your metrics and how you are tracking to your goals. And don't forget to translate your outcomes through some mathematical formulas that our finance folks have checked and that support our overall company goals.

John. Fantastic! I love the label 'CyberValue;' it's a great way to get our message to stick in the minds of our stakeholders and a provocative way to engage customers. I'll work with Susan on building the deck and, as you suggest, take the show on the road. We'll prepare a presentation that achieves the goals you've articulated.

Turning to Susan, John says: let's also take this opportunity to introduce the MEDDIC framework as part of our prescribed sales approach. So, let's include a slide or two to connect the dots between CVM and MEDDIC. Susan's presentation consists of a deck of slides as shown in the figure below with speaker notes.

Slide	Susan Smart's Speaker Notes
Today's Challenges	CyberSecure Challenges • Can't reach / gain attention of the Economic Buyer & Champion • Getting Buyer Team consensus on Why Change? Why Now? Why CyberSecure? • Discounting erodes quota attainment. Reps cannot have a business value conversation; hence price is the only leverage • Sales cycles are too long — which increases cost of sales and reduces first year revenue • Sales team quota attainment is too low — resulting in high sales team turnover • Inability to scale value selling practices to support a larger number of opportunities; thus, only a few large strategic deals can be supported. • Can't expand footprint through cross-sell / upsell because can't show value of current investment Buyer Challenges • Limited time to engage with salespeople; no interest in product functionality conversation • Economic Buyer skeptical about overly-simplistic calculators and lack of business case transparency • No budget for a new tool / automation platform – cybersecurity is a new requirement • Too difficult to overcome the inertia of the status quo... why should we go through the pain of change? • Unable to differentiate between competing vendor offers • Overwhelmed with data, yet unable to determine what is relevant to their specific situation • Economic Buyer insists on internal stakeholder consensus before investing • Cannot justify expanded footprint because they cannot measure and showcase value realized of current investment

Slide	Susan Smart's Speaker Notes
Vision: What Does a GREAT Buyer-Seller Experience Look Like	Characterize the nature of the transformation (Current State to Desired Future State). Paint the picture of what a better future looks like: CyberSecure Sales Team • Grab attention with provocative value hypothesis based on internal account team knowledge and industry benchmarks • Follow-up by engaging buyer team with credible process and methodology leading to defensible business case • Lock-in your relationship as Trusted Advisor by closing the loop through measuring and showcasing value realized post implementation — helping lock in renewals and set stage for account expansion Buyer Experience • Access to content that helps overcome the inertia to change – including 'No Decision' outcome • Credible way to justify budget and set priorities • Buy-in from stakeholders to support the investment decision • Proof that current investments are achieving original ROI expectations
Why a CyberValue Program	Buyers and Sellers are basically in the same boat. Cite IDC research: • 90% of buyers require quantifiable evidence of business benefits before investing • 2/3 of buyers confess to lacking the knowledge and tools to create a credible business case • 80% of buyers look to their suppliers for assistance in quantifying value The message to deliver is: 'Buyers want CyberSecure's help, so let's give it to them!'
CyberValue Program Focus	• The CyberValue Program: Collaboration between CyberSecure and Customers • The Goal: Provide sales teams with repeatable way to engage Economic Buyers in meaningful business value conversations – leading to a defensible, customer-specific business case and follow-on ability to measure value realized

Slide	Susan Smart's Speaker Notes
How do we get there?	High-level walk-through CyberValue Program implementation stages • Create CVM framework and data model • Customer validation • Sales Playbook and assets • Enablement
Sales Process / MEDDIC Alignment	Clarify alignment of CyberValue Program with the sales process and MEDDIC. Specifically, the program: • Gains credibility with Economic Buyer **(E)** and Champion **(C)** as Trusted Advisor • Generates Metrics **(M)** needed to justify investment and measure value realized post implementation • CyberSecure sales process is aligned with buyer process **(Dp)** and criteria **(Dc)** and provides input in the desired formats • Each Benefit in the Value Model features a quantifiable 'pain point **(Ip)** – value statement pair'
Potential Business Benefits (Industry benchmarks)	Cite industry research, such as these statistics from a Miller Heiman 2018 CSO Insight Report: • 44% increase Win rates • 28% reduced sales cycle • 28% increased average deal size • 27% reduced customer churn • 23% increased available selling time • 20% reduced salesperson ramp-up time • 5% reduced cost of sales
Open Dialogue	Summarize challenges, success factors, and discuss next steps

Just in case more detail is requested on the alignment of the CyberValue Program with MEDDIC, Susan is prepared to provide more detail as shown in Figure 2.5.

Align CVM with Other Prescribed Sales Frameworks

MEDDIC is not the only popular framework used by sales organizations to get across the importance of selling business value. Sandler, Miller Heiman, and the Challenger framework are other prescribed approaches. Regardless of the prescribed approach, it's important for you to connect the dots between the CVM engagement model and these frameworks.

Figure 2.5: Aligning CVM with MEDDIC

ATTRIBUTES	GOAL	CONSIDERATIONS	Attributes of CVM Program
M Metrics	Quantify and measure potential business value (business case)	Do you know what the true ROI and payback period will be on the project? Did they participate in building and do they agree with the ROI model? Have you transferred ownership to the EB?	Each Pain Point – Value Statement pair in the CVM value model is quantified using a formula consisting of three factors: Driver Factor, Financial Factor, Improvement Factor - ensuring total transparency of the numbers.
E Economic Buyer	Know the Economic Buyer	This is the person who owns the budget (or can create budget) for the solutions you are selling. Do you know who is influential? What are personal and professional interests in signing off on the deal?	As part of the qualification process, sales reps need to engage the EB at the outset to (a) sell the CVM process; (b) address concerns; (c) identify a buyer point of contact; and (d) gain buy-in to conduct the prescribed CVM exercise
DP Decision Process	Understand investment decision governance process	How are investment decisions made? Who is in the power base? Who will sign off on moving forward at each stage?	Sales reps need to emphasize that the CVM process is aligned with buyer process and provide input in the desired formats.
DC Decision Criteria	Understand technical and economic criteria	Did you set the success criteria, or did your competitor? Have you provided your prospect with a "lock out document" (set of capabilities used in evaluation)	As part of each Benefit, solution capabilities are associated with each pain point - value statement pair.
IP Identified Pain	Understand business pain driving the need for a Solution	Identify the pain — Is it measurable? Who benefits from fixing it? What happens if it's not fixed?	Each building block of the CVM framework is a 'pain point – value statement pair' – describing how value will be measured and contribute to addressing pain.
C Champion/ Coach	Line up a "coachable" Champion - willing and able to influence the decision	The person that you educate and who will fight for you when you are not in the room. Try to understand what the personal motivation and help them help you.	Sales reps need to sell the CVM Program to the Champion and coach this individual. Ideally, co-present results of the business case to the EB.

Gain executive sponsorship

If possible, your network of advocacy should include lining up key top business executives like the CEO and CFO. Perhaps the best way to do this is by aligning the CVM Program with planned or in-progress enterprise transformation initiatives.

Early stage companies typically gear their business models to address major industry trends. For example, cloud transformation has given rise to a host of new companies in the cybersecurity, IT service management, and DevSecOps marketspace. More mature companies, in addition to having to align with industry trends, may have enterprise-wide initiatives to renew their business models and practices. For example, enterprise-wide programs associated with 'lean principles' and quality-oriented processes (e.g., TQM, Six Sigma) are good candidates for connecting the dots with a CVM Program.

> Regardless of the enterprise transformation driver, having the CRO arrange a formal presentation to the CEO and CFO to get them on-board is very helpful and will accelerate advocacy.

Let's use our case study to explore this idea further.

CASE STUDY EPISODE 2: Lining Up CEO and CFO Support for a 'CyberValue Program'

At a recent Board Meeting, Justin Tyme, CyberSecure founder and CEO, and Lauren Profit, CFO, explained their business strategy: to become a dominant player in the Cloud Transformation security market space and position the company for an IPO within 3-5 years. They planned to do this by leveraging the paradigm shift and associated security challenges that enterprises face in connection with cloud transformation — since most global 2000 companies and major government agencies have invested heavily in securing the traditional corporate data center and are not prepared to secure their employees use of the internet against malware and phishing attacks.

To achieve their aggressive business goals, they recognized the need to accelerate profitable revenue growth by adding new customers and expanding revenue in existing customer accounts. John Cash was recently hired as CRO to make this happen.

John understood that getting both Justin and Lauren's support for the CyberValue Program would accelerate implementation. Among other things, John wanted a clear understanding of the potential obstacles he would have to deal with when the management team met to discuss budgets and investment funding priorities.

Given their diverse backgrounds and interests, John elected to engage Justin and Lauren in separate one-on-one briefings – using an abbreviated version of the stakeholder briefing described in Episode 1. Given their diverse backgrounds, Justin and Lauren shared some interesting perspectives on the CyberValue Program proposal.

Justin, given his more technical background and cybersecurity expertise, quickly understood why a CyberValue Program was needed, but was unsure of how to go about implementing one. He explained that quantifying cybersecurity business benefits is very difficult and customers might not be easily persuaded to assign a dollar value to mitigating risks (viz., preventing things that might happen). He clarified: *'cybersecurity is not like investing in an ERP or CRM system where there are clear benefits in terms of increased revenue and reduced cost of sales.'*

John responded that actually a CVM for the sales organization is akin to an ERP in a manufacturing environment. He suggested that Justin take a look at the logical value model that Susan had developed. It would help him understand that the CyberSecure solution could indeed be quantified in terms of both direct (cost reduction) and indirect (risk mitigation) benefits. Justin consented to reviewing the model.

While it took a few weeks for Justin to get back to John and Susan, his response was worth the wait. Given his technical understanding of the domain, Justin truly dug into each line item in the value model and had a few questions and suggestions. Here was his bottom line.

'I like this approach a lot and feel we have a good start with the many potential value points listed. The process of asking the customer to help us define value up front will help us tease out how they think about us, which is incredibly helpful to the qualification process.'

Interestingly, Justin downplayed the value of quantification and up-played the fact that the process would help **drive conversations** and **qualify opportunities**. John and Susan were delighted: getting Justin's input and endorsement was a large step in moving the CyberValue Program ball forward.

Lauren, on the other hand, accepted the premise that CVM could be done, but had a very different set of questions (perhaps typical of issues that you will get from other CFOs) as follows:

- We've already made investments in other sales tools. How can we be assured that the sales teams will use it?

- How is this going to help our reps carry on high-quality conversations with C-level economic buyers?

- Why would buyers believe a business case provided by our sales reps?

- How does it deal with different sales situations? Verticals? Different countries? Different use cases? How does it scale for buyer organizations of different size?

- How much will it cost to build this capability? Why can't we build this ourselves instead of buying something else? *'I believe one of my financial analysts could knock this out in a few days.'*

- What if the ROI for a given deal turns out to be too low or even negative? For example, wrong benefits; costs too high; deal not qualified?

Good questions. Let's return to our narrative to address them.

Addressing the 'Make versus Buy' Question

The CFO concerns expressed in the case study are often shared by other business executives. In a broader sense, the concerns center on the age-old 'build versus buy' decision. Specifically, why can't we build this capability using Excel spreadsheets? The short answer is: 'you can, BUT.' There are three key aspects to the 'BUT' response that merit explanation. One aspect has to do with the different model development *use cases.* The other dimensions have to do with managing *complexity and security*. Let's explore each.

Value Model Development Use Cases: the Excel versus Platform Automation Debate

Recall some of the questions that CFOs are likely to ask during the Sell It stage:

- "How much would it cost to build this capability? Why can't we build this ourselves in Excel?"

- How is this going to help our reps carry on high-quality conversations with C-level economic buyers? How can we be assured that the sales teams will use it?

- Why would buyers believe a business case provided by our sales reps?

- How does it deal with different sales situations? Different industries or size organizations? Different countries or use cases?

The context for these questions often boils down to a debate over whether using Excel spreadsheets is preferred over a more scalable automation platform approach. As it turns out, this is not a Hobson's 'take it or leave it' choice; there is room for both tools. It's simply a question of when in the evolution of the CVM Program each comes into play.

To clarify, let's elaborate on what goes on in the value model development and validation stages of the CVM Program implementation. Specifically, there are two interdependent use cases to consider. Excel works well in the first; it fails in the second.

1. **Value Model Content Development / Validation**. This stage is about developing the Value Data Model and validating it with customers. It includes precisely defining the universe of benefits associated with a B2B solution — focusing on the underlying 'pain point – value statement' pairs and the factors required to quantify them. The initial 'strawman' value model should be developed by capturing the collective knowledge of people internal to the B2B solution organization – across the sales, SE, marketing, and product management teams. For this activity, Excel serves as an excellent 'rapid prototyping' tool. The result of this stage can then be used to validate the strawman Value Model and outputs with 'friendly' customers.

2. **User Experience (UX) Validation**. The next stage of validation requires assessing the best way to implement the value model and associated assets in the steady state. Can the delivery of the Excel-based Value Model be scaled? Is it easy for the sales teams to use it? Does it support iterative refinement as you move through the sales cycle? Will customers accept the transparency and quality of the resulting deliverables? Can these outputs be quickly and efficiently re-generated during the business case refinement process? Here is where Excel falls short, and a CVM platform makes a tremendous difference.

The figure below highlights the key attributes and considerations involved in the Excel vs. automation platform debate.

Figure 2.6: Comparison of Approaches: Worksheets versus CVM Automation Platform

User Experience Attributes	Requirement	Excel	CVM Automation Platform
Customer Engagement Process Support	Full support of customer engagement cycle: Value Discovery- Value Delivery- Value Realization	◕ (partial)	● (full)
Scalability	Efficiency of refining / customizing business case through numerous iterations	◔ (partial)	● (full)
Single Source of Truth	Support for any language, currency, and number format in both UI and Content/Assets	○ (none)	● (full)
	Single master repository of value knowledge		
Flexibility / Adaptability	Support variety of sales situations accounting for geographical, industry, use cases, scale variations	◑ (partial)	● (full)
	Seamless integration of multiple solution models		
Usability	Ability to quickly adapt to business changes: new solutions; product enhancement; acquisitions, etc.	◔ (partial)	● (full)
	Usable by all sales reps for all qualified deals in the pipeline with basic business acumen; Contextual Help to promote adoption		
	Credible and transparent with customers; easy to refine and validate business case; clear on 'where numbers come from'		
Security	Full SOC Compliance; ensure security of all customer data	◔ (partial)	● (full)
Visibility across the enterprise	Executive access/ dashboards & measurement provide tracking usage and adoption information	○ (none)	● (full)
Value Realization Measurement	Periodic assessments of value achieved relative to the ROI baseline	○ (none)	● (full)
Integration to other enterprise apps	Integration with other processes and tools in the sales ecosystem (CRM, Customer Success)	○ (none)	● (full)

The table below expands on the rationale for the colored circles – providing a number of the considerations you should keep in mind when making the build versus buy assessment.

Figure 2.7: Considerations for Evaluating Automation Platforms

User Experience Attributes	Key Requirement	Considerations
Customer Engagement Process Support	Full support of customer engagement cycle: Value Discovery - Value Delivery - Value Realization	A CVM platform supports the full customer engagement cycle. Spreadsheets are typically geared to building a business case. They add little or no value to the Value Discovery or Value Realization stages
Scalability	Efficiency of refining / customizing business case through numerous iterations Support for any language, currency, and number format in both UI and Content/Assets	With Excel, making changes to a model during customization of the business case with the buyer requires time-consuming rework (hours to copy and paste from Excel to PPT and Word documents). A platform: • Automatically regenerates high-quality sales assets in seconds • Supports multiple language, currency, and number formats in both the UI and outputs • Captures and associates case studies with Benefits
Single Source of Truth	Single master repository of value knowledge	With Excel, an enterprise loses control of the message as different people end up with different iterations of the original spreadsheet and no one gets the latest information. A platform featuring a single repository of value is continuously updated.
Flexibility / Adaptability	Support variety of sales situations accounting for geographical, industry, use cases, and organization size / scale variations Seamless integration of business value across multiple solution models Ability to quickly adapt to business changes caused by adding new solutions; product enhancement; acquisitions, etc.	With Excel, dozens of spreadsheets are required to support variations. A platform configures deal-specific 'situations' in a single value model — permitting configuration and customization of the value model for each unique customer — accounting for industry, location, use case, and target audience variations. Business cases accounting for the integration of multiple solutions that may have overlapping benefits can be created to support real-world selling situations

User Experience Attributes	Key Requirement	Considerations
Usability	Usable by <u>all sales reps</u> with basic business acumen for <u>all qualified deals</u> in the pipeline	Spreadsheets typically rely on skilled Value Practitioners with deep understanding of the value model mechanics. Consequently, use of the spreadsheets are often constrained to the largest, most strategic deals.
	Contextual Help to promote adoption	An automation platform is specifically engineered for use by sales people – providing quick access to explanations and assistance to drive more effective adoption. Moreover, 'guided discovery' provides an efficient way to align benefits in the value model with business objectives and strategy
	Credible and transparent with customers; easy to refine and validate business case; clear on 'where the numbers come from'	
Security	Full SOC Compliance; ensure security of all customer data	Spreadsheets are generally difficult to control and risk exposing proprietary customer data and organizational IP to unauthorized access

A CVM platform provides the ability to leverage organizational IP and customer data in a secure manner and is accredited for full SOC compliance |
| Visibility across the enterprise | Executive access/ dashboards & measurement provide tracking usage and adoption information | Keeping track of who and how spreadsheets are used is cumbersome – requiring a separate tracking process, or not done at all.

An automation platform provides full visibility of adoption and usage by sales team members. A dashboard shows all business cases in process — highlighting sales team members that need guidance or further training |
| Value Realization Measurement | Periodic assessments of value achieved relative to the ROI baseline | An automation platform provides a value realization methodology as an integral part of full CVM life cycle support |
| Integration to other enterprise apps | Integration with other processes and tools in the sales ecosystem (CRM, Customer Success) | An automation platform provides APIs and is fully integrated with the current sales ecosystem including CRM, SSO, LMS, and other tools |

Lastly, in addition to use as a front-end prototyping tool, recognize that financial / accounting types may prefer Excel spreadsheets because they are used internally to justify other enterprise investments – so it is baked into the standard decision-making process and provides more visibility into the underlying business logic of the business case. This is why the CVM automation platform should also automatically generate Excel worksheets as another output.

In summary, Excel is useful as a helpful model prototyping tool, to initially load the baseline value model into the automation platform, and to provide financial types with visibility into the quantification logic for a business case. However, it does not pass the test of a secure, industrial-strength, sales self-service enterprise-scale application to support value selling in the steady state.

The requirements for scalability and dealing with complexity are so significant that they merit further discussion as follows.

Dealing with the Value Model Complexity Cube

To expand further on the issues of flexibility, adaptability, and scalability, recall that a single Solution Value Model consists of the core set of 'pain point – value statement pairs' that frame each individual benefit in the model. Each pair is quantified by a set of 'factors' (driver factor, financial factor, improvement factor, scaling factor). And at the 'model level' there are a number of other levers that can be used to customize a business case for a given customer (e.g., discount rate, benefit realization percent, etc.). In your library, this baseline value model represents a 'strawman' that needs to be configured for each unique customer situation.

But what happens to the values in the baseline model for these various factors when you engage buyers in different geographies, industries, or competitive alternatives? The values and assumptions in the baseline model will change, leading to a proliferation of models that target these different 'sales situations.'

The Value Model Complexity Cube (below) illustrates this challenge by examining the key 'dimensions' that drive customization of a business case for each unique deal. Specifically:

- Number of <u>solution models</u> to be invoked. Each proposal quantifies the value of 1-N solutions.

- Each Solution has 1-N <u>value statements</u> – each one quantified by a variety of <u>Factors:</u> driver factor, financial factor, improvement factor, and scaling factor (to accommodate different size organizations)

- The value statements selected and the factor values may vary for each unique <u>sales situation</u> – industry, geography, use case, competitors, etc.

Figure 2.8: The Value Model Complexity Cube

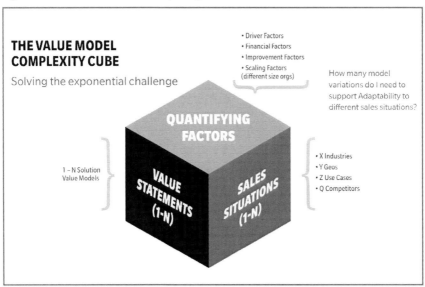

Thus, at a conceptual level, the 'Value Model Complexity Equation' requires building and maintaining an unmanageable number of individual models to support all the deals in the pipeline. You can think of the support requirement in terms of a Complexity Equation that leads to a maintenance nightmare.

Complexity Equation = # Solution Models * # Value Statements * # Factors * # Geos * # Industries * # Use Cases → Maintenance Nightmare

This requirement can be handled in one of 3 ways:

1. Build a baseline spreadsheet model for each Solution, then customize and refine it for each deal situation on-the-fly.

2. Build a complex homegrown model in Excel to address this requirement. This is (a) expensive to build and maintain, (b) error prone and difficult to use and secure, (c) requires high priced Business Value Consultants to explain and use, and (d) increases the risk of losing important, proprietary IP if these people leave the company (then what?)

3. Select a commercially available automation platform that does all this heavy lifting for you.

For most mid-size sales organizations, option 3 makes the most sense. A commercial off-the-shelf product has typically been built over a number of years by experts and reflects millions of dollars in investments. Why re-invent the wheel?

Certifying CVM Platform Security via SOC Compliance Audit

Lastly, keep in mind that the content in your CVM repository (value model and associated assets) represent an important source of your company's intellectual property (IP). Properly designed this IP differentiates your company from direct competitors and exposes your competitive sales strategy.

Maintaining this content in Excel models that are distributed across individual laptops makes it almost impossible to control quality and consistency of deliverables. It also raises the risk of this content being accidently or intentionally disclosed to competitors. Ask yourself: what if this IP leaves the company when a key person exits the company? What is your exposure to this threat? This is an important reason why a centrally controlled repository of CVM content is important.

> *An agile CVM platform should feature SOC 2 compliance – an auditing component using the American Institute of CPAs (AICPA)'s Service Organization Control reporting platform designed to ensure data security, minimal waste and shareholder confidence.*

Its goal is to ensure that systems are set up so they assure security, availability, processing integrity, confidentiality, and privacy of customer data. SOC 2 requirements are mandatory for all engaged, technology-based service organizations that store client information in the cloud. Such businesses include those that provide SaaS and other cloud services while also using the cloud to store each respective, engaged client's information.

PLAN IT – Best Practices to Ensure Stakeholder Commitment

Build a Plan that Shows How CVM Supports the Full Customer Value Cycle

The role of the Value Practitioner has traditionally been constrained to the *front-end* of the sales cycle (to building a business case to help sell solutions) or to salvage a deal in trouble – very often after the 'horse has already left the barn'. This approach sub-optimizes the contribution of the Value Practitioner.

Instead, an effective CVM Program Plan should support the full Customer Value Cycle – from Value Discovery to Value Delivery to Value Realization. To make this happen, the plan should address a few key issues:

- a. **WHY**. What are your enterprise business imperatives? Paint a vision of a better future state — including the measurable goals of a CVM Program.

- b. **WHY Now**. Create a sense of urgency. What opportunity are we missing?

- c. **WHY You**. Why are you in the best position to drive the program?

d. **HOW**. Provide a framework that clarifies how the program will be used to engage both *prospective buyers* in building a defensible business case and *existing customers* in measuring and showcasing value realized.

To address these questions, it's important to build a compelling business case as follows.

Use a Compelling Business Case to Set Expectations and Measurement Baseline

To get executive level buy-in to the CVM program, you should be prepared with a model that addresses the 'Why" and 'Why Now' questions in financial terms. Think of this as essentially an *'ROI for the ROI Program.'* Let's return to our CyberSecure Case Study, to see how Susan Smart (Value Practitioner) helped John Cash (CRO) justify the investment.

CASE STUDY EPISODE 3: Making the Business Case for the 'CyberValue Program'

Recall that CyberSecure is an early stage business in the cybersecurity market space with high-growth expectations. John Cash, it's newly appointed CRO, wants to transform its business from a technical product selling model to a value selling approach. At a Quarterly Business Review (QBR) with the regional vice presidents, he (with Susan's assistance) communicates the following high-level transformation vision.

Figure 2.9: Painting a Customer Value Management Vision for a Better Future

CURRENT STATE	DESIRED FUTURE STATE
• Early stage start-up mode with aggressive sales team ramp-up goals; need ability to scale quickly • Generic solution selling (as opposed to a differentiated business value selling approach) • QBR feedback from sales managers. Recognized challenge internally with having business value conversations with customers and then presenting business value / ROI to them • No scalability. Current Excel-based is only used for small fraction of deals in pipeline (requires too much value consulting expertise) • Renewal rates below expectations	Enable entire sales channel to carry on effective value conversations through the complete customer engagement cycle. Specifically: • Gain Economic Buyer buy-in to collaborate on a business case • Frame value proposition in a quantifiable way • Engage buyer team to discover required data and assumptions • Present a defensible business case to the Economic Buyer (leading to transfer of ownership of the business case) • Measure value realized post implementation to ensure renewals and position upsell / cross-sell opportunities.

John asks Susan to build a 'bullet-proof' business case to justify investing in the CyberValue Program. Here's the methodology Susan uses.

1. Agree with John on the performance metrics that he views as critical to the CVM investment decision. John decides that there are two key metrics:
    a. Increase win rate
    b. Reduce discounting leading to Higher Average Deal size

2. Characterize current state situation and planned growth
    a. Number of sales reps (FTE) = 20; growing to 30 in Year 2 and 40 in year 3
    b. Average deal size = $150,000
    c. Average annual number of deals closed / rep = 8

3. Build ROI model that provides John and his team with 'levers' to assess the impact of different assumptions. For example
   a. Win rate increase = 10%
   b. Discount rate reduction (Average Deal Size uplift) = 5%
   c. Discount rate (for calculating Net Present Value) = 12%
   d. CVM annual subscription cost per user = $1000
   e. CVM services cost (implementation and training) = $50,000 (one-time)

Figure 2.10: Justifying CVM Investment (a Business Case Example)

	NPV	Year 1	Year 2	Year 3
REVENUE				
• Current State Revenue	$ 11,801,020	$ 3,000,000	$ 4,500,000	$ 6,000,000
• Future State Revenue	$ 12,391,071	$ 3,150,000	$ 4,725,000	$ 6,300,000
A. Projected Revenue Increase	$ 590,051	$ 150,000	$ 225,000	$ 300,000
COST				
• CVM SW Cost	$ 78,673	$ 20,000	$ 30,000	$ 40,000
• CVM Services Cost	$ 50,000	$ 50,000	$ -	$ -
B. Projected Costs	$ 128,673	$ 70,000	$ 30,000	$ 40,000
Net Benefit (NPV) = A minus B	$ 461,378			
ROI= [(A-B)/B] * 100%	359%			

This initial projection shows an ROI in excess of 300%. This may be high – especially given the fact that only 2 potential benefits are quantified. However, John and team understand that this provides a reasonable, directional sense of potential business value. Susan is given the green light to build out the required content and infrastructure.

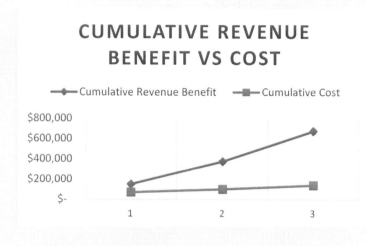

BUILD IT – Best Practices to Create Reusable, Easy-to-Use Content

The Build It stage requires developing content at the right 'altitude' for the right people and providing an automation capability featuring ease of use, scalability, and adaptability to a variety of deal situations. Because the Solution Value Model is the centerpiece of the CVM Program, we begin by clarifying what an effective value model looks like.

Use the Solution Value Data Model as the CVM Centerpiece

The Solution Value Model(s) is the collection of benefits that constitutes the content foundation for the CVM Program. It is critical to every stage of the CVM journey – creating a value hypothesis with your internal account team; building and refining a defensible business case with the buyer team; measuring value realized post solution implementation; and creating persona relevant assets along the way.

Sellers often struggle with the challenge of connecting their buyer's challenges (pain points) to the business value of their B2B solutions. Inability to do this may lead to a credibility gap — providing numbers without context. Overly simplistic ROI Calculators fail to bridge this gap; in fact, they may widen the gap. While calculators may be a provocative way to open the door and generate leads, they fail to provide the rigor required to justify an investment in a B2B solution. Thus, the challenge is: how do you build a value model that can both be used to generate interest (with a provocative value hypothesis); then move on to refine the hypothesis into a compelling business case; and finally close the loop by using the baseline model to measure value realized. The answer is: build a rigorous Value Data Model with the ability to abstract data to suit a variety of needs. Let's explore the practical implications of this statement.

The Value Model is a collection of *precisely-defined* benefits that constitute the baseline financial model to be used and customized by sales reps in building a unique business case for each customer. It provides Economic Buyers with the ability to assess alternative scenarios from worst to best case — performing sensitivity analyses, observing the impact of possible risk factors, answering 'what if' questions, and projecting a variety of financial factors (e.g., ROI, NPV, payback, etc.) for a proposed investment.

So, what is a precisely-defined benefit? A benefit is the fundamental building block of a value model. Think of it as the 'atomic unit' of business value that provides the buyer and seller with the wherewithal to assemble a customized business case for a B2B solution. A well-defined, reusable benefit consists of the following elements.

- Benefit Name. A label that communicates how a specific driver's improvement is quantified in terms of its business impact. For example: does it reduce costs, improve productivity, mitigate risk; etc.

- Description. A narrative that provides (a) context for the benefit by characterizing the nature of pain and (b) a brief value statement communicating specifically how business value is quantified. For example, will it reduce the time and effort associated with a given activity (e.g., problem resolution); displace software license costs; reduce customer churn.

- <u>Capability</u>. Describes the use cases or specific features of a solution offering associated with the value statement claim.

- <u>Proof Points</u>. Specific evidence that supports the value statement claim, typically in the form of either (a) first-hand customer experience (value realized) with the B2B solution capability and / or (b) industry analyst benchmark data.

- <u>Value Calculation</u>. Three factors used to quantify each value statement, including:

  - *Driver Factor*. A key measure of business success or business risk that the solution contributes to or mitigates. For example: Number of Security Incidents; Number of IT Staff; Number of Software Licenses.

  - *Financial Factor*. A value that monetizes the calculation — typically expressed as a Labor rate, Unit Cost, or Unit Revenue.

  - *Improvement Factor*. A range of expected improvement associated with the Driver factor (Conservative – Probable – Aggressive) which may be expressed in percentage terms or absolute numbers.

The figure below provides an example of a Benefit defined for a cybersecurity solution. The complete collection of Benefits characterized in this way constitutes the Value Model for the cybersecurity solution.

Benefit Name. Reduce Web Site Malware Containment Costs

Description. Allowing users to visit a wide variety of sites across different categories is a business imperative, yet it introduces significant risk and financial burden to the organization. Our solution reduces Security Operations Engineer labor costs associated with web malware containment

Capability. Isolation prevents active web content reaching the end-point, thus sites across a wide array of categories, including uncategorized web sites, present zero risk.

Proof Points. *Ponemon Institute: The Cost of Malware Containment, January 2015*: A Financial Services institution found >60% infections due to uncategorized web sites and that average enterprise spends 600 hrs. / week on malware containment. Considering that the average hourly cost of a security operations center (SOC) engineer is $82, the cost comes to more than $2.5 million annually.

Value Calculation
SOC-engineer-FTE * Fully Burdened SOC Engineer Salary * Percent Improvement

5 FTE * $170,000 * 50% = $425,000 / year (cost reduction)

Benefits defined in this way can be grouped or aggregated in various ways. These logical groupings represent abstractions of the value model that can be used to communicate value to different buyer personas. We will expand on this subject in a subsequent section of the book addressing persona-relevant content.

Prescribe a Buyer Engagement Process for Both Prospective Buyers and Existing Customers

With the Value Data Model as the 'center of gravity' for the CVM Program, the buyer engagement process is illustrated and described below.

Figure 2.13: The Value Data Model as the Centerpiece of the Customer Engagement Process

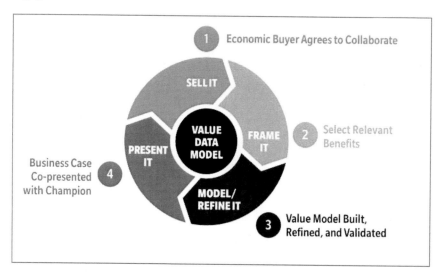

Here's how it works.

1. SELL IT requires engaging a buyer (or existing customer) to gain agreement on collaboration. As we shall see in Part 3 of this book, there is some homework that you'll need to do in advance of engaging the customer to properly open the door to the Economic Buyer and set the stage for the collaborative value modeling exercise.

2. FRAME IT involves selecting the subset of benefits from the value model that you feel resonate with the buyer. Keep in mind that the value model represents the 'universe' of potential benefits for a solution. Usually, a subset of benefits will suffice for a specific customer business case.

3. **MODEL / REFINE IT** reflects the idea that building a business case is an iterative process. First, the Value Data Model is used to build a strawman Value Hypothesis with your internal account team. This version of the model is then used as a provocative way to gain buyer attention and agreement to collaborate on refining the model. It demonstrates that you've done your homework and are ready to have a meaningful value conversation value. This Value Hypothesis is then refined with the buyer's team to reflect their data and assumptions. Typically, this exercise involves a group of 'decision influencers' on the buyer's team and requires a number of iterations to generate a final, compelling business case.

4. **PRESENT IT** involves packaging the final business case for presentation. Ideally, getting your Champion to co-present the business case with you makes it clear to the Economic Buyer that there is team consensus on the result. The goal of this step is to <u>transfer ownership</u> of the business case to the Economic Buyer, getting his / her agreement to recommend the investment to their governance board.

Part 3 of this book will drill down into more detail on each step and provide examples of outputs. At this point, we can turn our attention to the required enterprise-scale tool set to deliver each of these steps consistently and repeatably.

Implement Enterprise-scale Automation

Over the past two decades the increased emphasis on a value-selling sales model has led to significant commercial investments and improvements in automated tools. What was once a 'back-of-the-napkin' conversation between seasoned sales reps and buyers, evolved to Excel spreadsheets that required experienced ROI gurus to customize for each large deal, to the need for an enterprise scale value automation platform. As already mentioned, B2B software companies are finding that while Excel spreadsheets have their use, an effective automation platform is required to ensure secure, enterprise-wide scalability and flexibility to support a variety of sales situations.

As previously discussed, spreadsheets are helpful on the front-end for rapid prototyping a Value Model and perhaps on the back-end to satisfy the needs of procurement types. But they fail to provide the scalability and usability required to support sales teams. Hence, it's important to consider replacing homegrown processes and tools with an effective Customer Value Management automation platform, including an integrated set of applications that supports the full customer engagement life cycle; specifically:

- *Value Discovery*. Both the buyer and seller need a reason to initiate a meaningful conversation. Buyers need a value hypothesis: *'given your understanding of our business challenges, what is the potential business value of your solution?'* Sellers need an efficient way to (1) gain unique insights into the buyer's business needs; (2) reach the Economic Buyer to reframe the conversation around potential business outcomes; and (3) quantify a *value hypothesis* in terms of a projected baseline value model.

- *Value Delivery* involves collaborating with the buyer's team to determine which solution benefits are relevant to the modeling exercise and quantifying them with buyer-provided data and assumptions. The goal: create a transparent business case, transfer ownership to the Economic Buyer, and implement the B2B solution successfully setting the stage for periodically quantifying value achieved. This stage usually includes a Proof of Value and ends with the successful implementation of the B2B solution in the customer's environment.

- *Value Realization* requires measuring actual value realized (against the projected ROI baseline) and showcasing results. This stage should lead to a satisfied customer — helping lock-in renewals and creating opportunities to cross-sell and upsell solutions.

In summary, effective CVM automation features a self-service, secure, software-enabled platform that:

(1) promotes scalability, repeatability, maintainability, and consistency across the full customer engagement life cycle;

(2) provides a 'single source of truth' with respect to communicating business value;

(3) aligns with your prescribed sales process (including frameworks like MEDDIC, Challenger, Miller Heiman)[1] and go-to-market strategy; and

(4) provides a predictable / efficient engagement model that allows customers to "critique" rather than "create from scratch" required deliverables – minimizing the time and effort required for buyers to engage, validate and take ownership of the output.

Figure 2.14 provides a checklist of CVM automation platform capabilities that elaborate on these requirements.

---

[1] Note: Sales frameworks explain WHAT to do, but not HOW to do it. An effective CVM process provides a prescriptive way to engage customers with appropriate scripts and supporting sales assets.

Figure 2.14: Checklist of CVM Automation Platform Requirements

CUSTOMER VALUE MANAGEMENT PLATFORM	CAPABILITIES AND FEATURES
Responsiveness	Any connected device supported, Mobile, Tablet, Desktop, etc.
Localization	Any language, currency, and number format both UI and Content/Assets
CRM Integration	Salesforce.com Sales Cloud, Microsoft CRM Dynamics, and more
SSO Integration	SAML 2.0, VMWare Workspace One, Okta
Data Integration	Universal Data Approach with standard integration with reliable sources
LMS Integration	Access to prescribed Learning Management System
Logging & Reporting	Full analytics, logging and auditing for administrators and users
Dynamic Content Assets	Quickly, easily, dynamically create fully branded MS Office or PDF assets
Sharing	Share solutions with partners. Share positions, props and realizations with customers
Cloning	Clone solutions, positions, props, and realizations to support unlimited scenarios
Best Practice Libraries	Solution Models, Content / Assets Templates, etc.
Internal and Community Forums	Collaborate and share best practices with other value sellers
Contextual Help	Quick access to explanations and assistance to drive more effective adoption
SOC Compliance	Compliance with American Institute of CPAs Service Organization Control reporting platform
API	Programmatic access to all aspects of CVM Platform
Value Models	
Solution Differentiation	Differentiate your solution(s) and the benefit(s) you provide
Solution Combinations	Combine multiple solutions together to support real-world selling situations
Standardized Benefit Formulas	Straightforward, standard calculation approach that allows sellers and buyers to get on the same page fast
Multi-Dimensional Situations	Change you value profile based on customer industry, location, use case, audience, etc.
Supporting Collateral Links	Link to collateral like pitch decks, analyst reports, and other marketing materials
Embedded Case Studies / References	Defend your value with materials in your sales library
Advanced Calculations	All the flexibility of a spreadsheet without the danger of "formula fatigue"

CUSTOMER VALUE MANAGEMENT PLATFORM	CAPABILITIES AND FEATURES
Value Insights	
Data Aggregation and Analysis	Data pulled from web, paid, primary, and algorithmic sources
Data Visualization	Peer performance comparisons and automated balance sheet analysis of prospects
Value Positions	
Guided Discovery	Steps to effectively capture the customers pain and drive toward solutioning
Quick Value Hypothesis'	In a couple clicks create an "outside-in" perspective of your value for any customer
Account Based Marketing Support	Leverage Value Positions in outbound marketing campaigns with tailored value
Value Propositions	
Supports Real-World Selling Scenarios	Leverage all your internal knowledge and dynamically apply it simply and dynamically
Supports All Major CFO Hurdle Rates	Total Benefits, ROI, NPV, IRR, Payback Period, 3 Month Cost of Inaction, TCO, and more
Supports Total Cost of Ownership	Facilitate the simplest of ROI conversations by comparing current costs to "after" costs
Benefit Phasing	Consider customer current state and gradual realization of value over time
Internal and Customer Notations	Capture notes and context during engagement with a customer
Adapt to Customer Conversations	Add benefits and change the naming / descriptions to reflect customer preference
Differentiate from Alternatives	Support the fact that most customers are not "green field" opportunities
Value Realization	
Measure Expectation vs. Actual	Survey customers monthly, quarterly or annually for their perspective of value achieved
Facilitate Course Correction	In areas where value is not up to par, suggestions of potential changes to get on track
Capture Case Study Content	Capture quotes and other case study data to make your value case stronger going forward
Automatically Inform Value Models	Based on customer perspective, revise and refine your Value Models

Create High-quality, Persona-relevant Content

Agile customer value management has another important dimension to consider – specifically, that the outputs generated along the journey must satisfy the needs of different buyer and customer personas. As one Software Company COO puts it: *'Value content must be packaged at the right altitude, for the right people, at the right time.'*

There are also ways to create this content to help with its consistency and ease of use. In this section, we explain what content to develop and some of the nuances associated with creating it.

Sales Assets Should Support the Complete Customer Engagement Journey

To begin, it's important to understand precisely what specific knowledge needs to be created. To this end, it's helpful to think in terms of the objectives associated with the customer value journey.

As the figure below suggests, content is needed to:

- *gain insights* into a prospective buyer's situation
- *open doors* to buyer decision makers
- establish *credibility* as a Trusted Advisor
- *close deals* by engaging buyer teams to build a defensible business case
- *grow an account* by measuring and showcasing value realized to justify expansion.

Keeping these objectives and the targeted buyer personas in mind, we can create a list of the sales assets and collateral that should be created.

Figure 2.15: Sales Assets and Collateral that Drive Meaningful Conversations throughout the Customer Value Journey

Objective	Description
Gain insight to prospective buyer's situation	Sales assets to help gain knowledge of a specific industry and the target account's business situation. • Company Research Brief • Peer Comparison Analysis • Competitive SWOT Analysis • Industry Case Studies / Research
Open doors to decision makers	Assets that provide a reason for starting a conversation and show evidence that you have knowledge and insights to share that their peers have found helpful – specifically a rigorous process and methodology that helps justify technology investments. • CVM Elevator Pitch. Major points to make when introducing the CVM Program to a prospect. • Customer Data Sheet Handout. One-page handout providing overview of the CVM Program — how it works and benefits to customer. • FAQ 1: Objection Handling. Suggested responses to typical buyer questions who may be skeptical about collaborating with a vendor on a business case. • Customer CVM Program Introductory briefing (PPT). Slides used to introduce the CVM process and methodology to the buyer (Economic Buyer, Champion, and decision influencers).
Establish credibility as Trusted Advisor	To launch meaningful value-centric conversations with your Economic Buyer and Champion, assets that help properly package your insights and account knowledge • Value Hypothesis. In a single page, a coarse 'directional' estimate of your solution's business value to the buyer – demonstrating that you've done your homework and that collaborating on a business case represents a potential win-win opportunity. • Value Pyramid. Based on research (e.g., Annual Report, Letter to shareholders, 10-K's / 10-Q's, Press Releases), a single page business summary of your account knowledge, including: Buyer Corporate Objectives, Business Strategies, Business / IT Initiatives, Risks & Critical Capabilities, & Summary of Solution Value • Value Statement Checklist. A list of 'pain point – value statement' line items used to engage customers in business value conversations – including data collection requirements.

Objective	Description
Close deals with defensible business case	Assets designed to target different buyer personas (C-levels, VP/ Directors, and Operational managers); provide the transparency required to support and defend your business case; and transfer ownership of the resulting business case to the Economic Buyer • Value Discovery Questions and assumptions. List of questions to capture the data and assumptions required to populate the value model with buyer data • Business Case Detail. Word document that contains all the benefits selected by buyer with supporting detail, including benefit description, capabilities, proof points, and assumptions for all quantification factors • Business Case Presentation Template (PPT). Slide set summarizing results of business value modelling exercise. • FAQ 2: Responses to Economic Buyer during presentation. Suggested responses to typical Economic Buyer questions asked during presentation of the final business case. • Spreadsheet version of business case. Excel version of business case for finance and procurement people
Expand account through cross-sell / upsell	Assets designed to measure and showcase value realized; lock-in renewals; shut out competitors; open doors to further cross-sell and upsell opportunities; and provide the Customer Success Team with an ROI baseline for periodic value assessment • Value Realization Survey • Value Realized Assessment Report • Case Study Content

Because the value model is central to the development of many of these assets, it deserves a few further words on its creation — specifically, some of the considerations in how to define and quantify benefits efficiently and consistently.

The Nuances of Identifying and Naming Benefits and Factors

Earlier in this book, we characterized the elements of a precisely-defined benefit. In this section, we drill down a bit further to provide some 'tips' on how you (a) identify the set of benefits that comprise a value model and (b) how you can use syntax to name benefits and factors to ensure consistency across different value models and make the result easy to communicate and understand.

We introduced the 'Driver Factor' as one of the three variables used to quantify a specific benefit in the value model. Recall, that the driver factor represents something measurable that is of key interest to the management of the business. You may wonder, *'is there a logical way to think through the driver factors that make most sense for a specific solution value model?'* Here's one way to do it.

Specifically, it may be helpful to think of driver factors in terms of a hierarchical data model. At the highest level (Level 1) are subject areas — 'things that matter' to a business that need to be managed effectively. Consider the following list as a starting point for your deliberations.

- **Assets.** Resources owned or leased by a company that have future economic value and can be measured in dollar terms.

- **Budget Line Items.** The cost and revenue related line items in an organization's annual budget that must be managed.

- **Customers.** Any buyer of a product or service offering that affects revenue and costs of an enterprise.

- **Events**. A one-time or repeatable occurrence that is sufficiently noteworthy to measure and record.

- **Incidents**. An occurrence or happening, possibly as a result of something else, that requires a response / resolution by either a person or machine that is measurable in terms of business value. (An incident, in the context of information technology, is an event that is not part of normal operations that disrupts operational processes.)

- **Locations**. A physical place of work (e.g., bank branches, warehouse locations)

- **Partner.** A commercial entity with which another commercial entity has some form of business relationship.

- **People**. A type of labor that performs a defined role to deliver measurable business value and receives compensation in terms of salary, hourly rate, or commission.

- **Products**. An item that is produced using enterprise resources (labor or capital) and offered for sale. Every product is made at a cost and sold at a price; thus, it has measurable economic value

- **Programs**. An initiative with a particular long-term aim providing measurable economic business value to the enterprise.

- **Projects**. A work effort that usually involves research, design, development, and / or implementation; requires a significant investment of time, is temporary in that it has a specified beginning and end time (and therefore defined scope and resources); and provides measurable economic business value to the enterprise.

- **Transactions**. An economic event with a third party that is measurable in money as a unit cost and recorded in an organization's accounting system.

- **Users**. Any consumer of a provider's products or services.

- **Vendors.** Provider of products or services

- **Applications.** Any software or set of computer programs used by business users to a business function.

By drilling down from these Level 1 subject areas, we can expose the list of driver factor 'candidates' that may be helpful in framing the value model. The illustration below shows how this is done for the 'Assets' subject area.

Figure 2.16: Example of Driver Factor Hierarchy

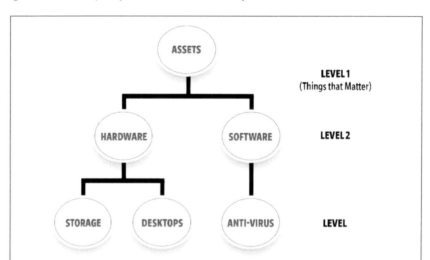

It's up to you and your stakeholders to determine what level of abstraction is appropriate. But the hierarchy provides you with a sound basis for having this conversation.

Use 'Concatenation' to Name Benefits and Identify Financial Factors

Syntax matters. Even after you have identified the appropriate set of driver factors for your value model, it's quite easy to get 'wrapped around the axle' when trying to come up with a consistent, thorough approach to naming benefits and identifying the associated financial factors. The use of a consistent approach and syntax for naming benefits and financial factors can significantly enhance the understandability of your value model. Here are some tips to help in this regard.

Naming Benefits. Recall that we defined a 'Benefit Name' as a label that communicates how a specific driver's improvement is measured in terms of its business impact. For example: does it reduce costs, improve productivity, mitigate risk; increase revenue. Let's expand further on another important consideration in naming benefits – specifically, by simply 'concatenating' Driver Factor and Business Impact Type. The table below illustrates how this is done.

Note how the Driver Factor appears in all Benefit names – either in the middle or the end of the name. It is qualified by Impact Type and the use of an 'Improvement verb type' (e.g., Reduce, Improve, Mitigate, Increase)

Figure 2.17 Naming Benefits by Concatenating Driver Factor with Business Impact Type

Business Impact Type	Beginning	Middle	End
Cost	Reduce	**Driver Factor** (e.g., Compromised Endpoint Reimaging)	Cost
Productivity	Improve	**Driver Factor**	Productivity
Risk	Mitigate	**Driver Factor**	Risk
Revenue	Increase / Protect Revenue	By Improving / Reducing	**Driver Factor**
Profit	Increase / Protect Profit	By Improving / Reducing	**Driver Factor**

By taking this approach you can quickly (and consistently) generate a starter set of benefits that should be considered for inclusion in your value model.

Identifying Financial Factors by Concatenation. Perhaps you've extended the above thinking to its logical conclusion. That's right, an associated set of Financial Factors can also be derived by 'concatenating' each Driver Factor with an appropriate 'monetizer.'

Figure 2.18: Naming Financial Factors using Concatenation

Monetizer	Driver Factor (Level 1)	Example
Cost per	Transaction Type	Cost per Malware Incident
Annual Burdened Salary	Person Type	Annual Burdened Salary Cybersecurity Engineer
Annual Spend for	Vendors	Annual Spend for Consulting Support
Annual Revenue per	Customer	Annual Revenue per Banking Customer

One clarifying point: the monetizer is also qualified by time period (e.g., hourly, monthly, yearly, occurrence).

Using Value Cards as a Conceptual Representation of a Benefit

Some organizations have found the use of a 'Value Card' as a helpful way of representing a Benefit – especially when you are introducing the program and engaging internal stakeholders to collaborate on the model building exercise.

The concept is that a Value Model can be represented as a 'deck' of cards. A sales rep would work with a buyer to select from the deck only those 'cards' that are relevant to their business case, and for which they are ready, willing, and able to provide the data and assumptions to override the factor values in the model.

As illustrated below, the Value Card is essentially a way of representing the 'meta model' for a benefit.

Figure 2.19: Using the 'Value Card' as a Conceptual Representation of a Benefit

Benefit Name	Pain Point	Value Category
Reduce Malware Remediation Cost	Current systems fail to provide protection from the increase in new attack vectors. Perimeter Security solutions such as Firewalls, Anti-Virus and IDS/IPS systems are not stopping the ever-evolving cyber threats.	**SOC Event Efficiency**
Capability	Isolation's ensures that no active web content reaches the end-point. The user's session and all active content (e.g. Java, Flash, etc.), whether good or bad, is fully executed and contained in the isolation platform	
Proof Point	ABC Financial Services Company reports zero malware infections from browsers or attachments	
Calculation		
# Endpoints Affected by Malware Attacks	52	
Cost per Malware Attack per Endpoint	$ 2,000	
Probable % Improvement	70%	
Expected annual savings	$ 72,800	
Benefit Type	**Direct**	
Impact Type	**Cost**	

The FTE Efficiency Gain Versus the Cost Per Event Trade-off

Most value models will include one or more benefits for labor cost savings or productivity improvement. Generally speaking, there are two ways to approach this subject: (1) use *FTE Labor Efficiency* gain for the relevant role(s) (e.g., cybersecurity engineer, help desk staff, etc.) or (2) quantify the benefit in terms of a *Cost per* Event, Incident, or Process Step that specific roles are engaged in. There are a few considerations that may help decide which route to take.

For models where a given role or labor category (e.g., cybersecurity engineer) is involved in multiple processes (hunting, problem identification, image data analysis, fixing problems, etc.) and handles a variety of different event types (alert analysis, malware remediation, phishing remediation) you should consider using 'Cost per' as a financial factor. Two reasons:

1. <u>Granularity and benchmark data availability</u>. You may want to highlight and quantify which specific steps in a full end-to-end process your solution adds value. Take for example a value model that seeks to quantify the value of efficiency gains for a Security Operations Center (SOC). As illustrated below, the incident response cycle consists of a number of steps – first steps to identify and classify the severity of the problem; second fixing the problem (or closing it as a false positive). SOC engineer labor is required across this cycle.

Figure 2.20: Clarifying Process Efficiency Gains

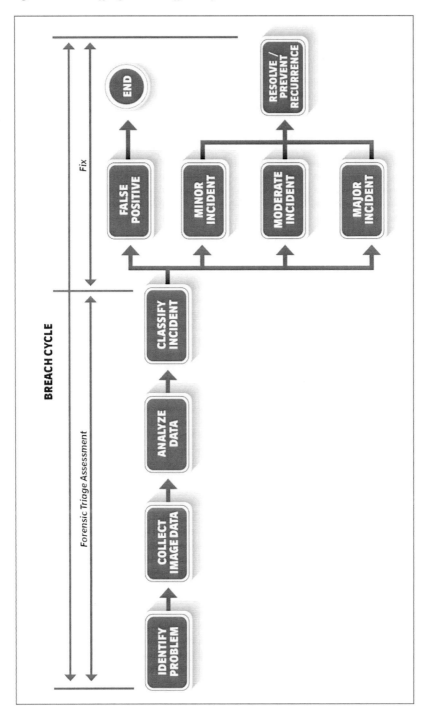

From a value modeling perspective, you have a number of choices:

a. Use percent FTE labor savings. For example: 10% SOC FTE time is currently spent on identifying the problem and collecting image data; 30% on analyzing data; 40% on fixing the problem; and 20% on other activities.

    i.   In this instance, you may decide to use SOC FTE as your driver factor to calculate the business value of improving the 'fixing the problem' activity. Thus, for example: 1 SOC FTE * 2080 hours per year * 40% = 832 hours per year)

    ii. Then: you may apply an improvement factor that indicates the level of productivity improvement that can be obtained on that portion of time (e.g.: 50% reduction in time required to "fix the problem"). When doing this, you need to clarify what you are impacting through the improvement. Are you reducing the time required to fix the problem? Or are you reducing the number of problems that occur? Both answers could apply; therefore, clearly specifying what is being impacted in your improvement factor is important to explaining and defending the calculation.

    iii. Lastly, for your financial factor, you would likely use Fully Burdened Cost per Hour for SOC FTE (e.g., Fully Burdened Annual Salary = $200,000 / 2080 hours per year = $96.15 per hour)

    iv. Thus, the benefit calculation is:

Driver Factor	Improvement Factor	Financial Factor	Annualized Savings
832 SOC FTE hours (fixing problems) *	50% Problem Fix Improvement *	$96.15 per SOC FTE hour	= $39,998

b. Use cost per event (or process step) as the metric. For example: $100 / triage event; $500 / fix

    i. In this instance, the driver factor is 'Number of Problem Fix Events per Year.' Thus: estimated annual number of "problems to fix" = 1 per week * 52 weeks per year = 52 problem fix events per year)

    ii. Then: apply an improvement factor indicating reduction in cost per event. For example: 50% reduction in cost to "fix the problem"

    iii. Lastly, for the financial factor, you elect to use an estimated cost per event. For example: assume each event requires 16 hours of effort to resolve at a fully burdened hourly rate of $96.15 per hour (calculated as shown above), for a total cost per event of 16 * 96.15 = $1538.40

    iv. Thus, the benefit value calculation is:

Driver Factor	Improvement Factor	Financial Factor	Annualized Savings
52 Problem Fix Events per Year *	50% Problem Fix Cost Reduction *	$1538.40 per Problem Event Fix	$39,998

Ultimately, the decision depends on (a) which steps in the process your solution addresses and (b) the availability of data to support your value statement claim. In general, event-based benefit calculations tend to be more readily accepted by customers because the factors are a bit more tangible; thus, may be easier to agree on the level of impact. However, many processes do not lend themselves to a discrete event type of analysis, in which case a productivity improvement on a portion of time may be more appropriate. If available Industry benchmark data is only available for the entire incident handling process (full breach cycle) or for key selected process steps (e.g. triage), then you might elect to use it.

Earlier we characterized Benefits as the 'atomic units' of business value for a given solution. As such, the illustration below shows that Benefits, as the fundamental building blocks of a Value Model, typically target the lower operational levels of the organization.

As you move up a buyer's organizational hierarchy, benefits are 'rolled up' and aggregated into other information categories designed to address different personas. For example, mid-level managers may want to know how the solution contributes to their Key Performance Indicators (KPIs) or whether benefits in the model are hard (direct) or soft (indirect). While C-levels are typically interested in understanding how a solution impacts the key business outcomes (Cost, Revenue, Productivity, Risk).

An effective value automation platform should deliver this information seamlessly – ensuring complete traceability of all metrics from the highest-level ROI and payback period down to the individual benefits from which these metrics are built.

Figure 2.21: Satisfying the Different Buyer Persona Information Needs

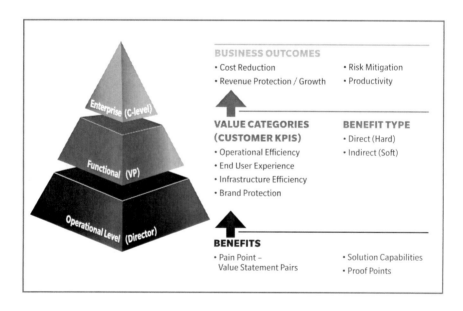

Customer Validation Before CVM Go-live

With a value model in hand, sales assets that support the complete customer engagement cycle, and an effective CVM delivery platform in place, you are now ready to engage 'friendly' current customers in a pilot program to collect feedback.

Customer validation should help to ensure that the CVM process and assets align and support the preferred way customers justify investments and showcase value realized. If possible, it's helpful to get customer feedback in both one-on-one customer engagements as well as in a group setting (perhaps using a Customer Advisory Group meeting as a possible venue).

Regardless of venue, consider the following topics and suggested messaging as a starting point for an agenda.

- **CVM Program Objectives**. Emphasize that the program is a collaboration between your company and a customer — designed to quantify and showcase the business value of your B2B solutions. Deliver the message that: The Program was created to respond to customers requesting assistance in quantifying and showcasing business value of our solutions. As such, there are two use cases for the Value Model that you will introduce: (1) for prospective buyers, to project expected business value and establish an ROI baseline against which value realized can be measured and (2) for existing customers, to measure and showcase value realized

- **Program Overview**. Use the schematic illustrated previously that shows your value model as the centerpiece of the program surrounded by the key engagement steps for Frame It, Model It, Refine It, Present It.

- **Value Model Overview**. Provide the list of benefits covered in the model and the 'meta model 'used to precisely define each individual benefit. The concept of a 'Value Card' introduced earlier may be helpful in this regard.

- **Demonstration**. 'Show and tell' the CVM platform navigation and outputs generated.

- **Engagement Process**. Use a table (like the figure below) to clarify how the engagement process would work along with the required customer resource commitment.

Figure 2.22: Example of Customer Validation Steps and Timetable

Step	Activities	Customer Resources	Staff Hours	Time Table
FRAME IT	Program Introduction and Workshop Kick-off; Present process to customer team; Customer team selects relevant benefits	Customer Team (Lead + stakeholders with your B2B solution experience)	2-3 hour working session	Day 1: 2 hour working session
MODEL IT	You build 'backward-looking' strawman model; (Original State vs Current State) with placeholder data and assumptions	NA	NA	Week 1
REFINE IT	Customer overrides placeholder values with their data	Customer Team	8 staff-hours	Week 2
PRESENT IT	You package and present results	Customer Team	2-hour session * # Team Members	Week 2

- Benefits of participating in program. Emphasize that the collaboration process:

  ○ Applies a proven methodology with minimal impact on customer's time and resources

  ○ Quantifies business value in a credible, transparent way

  ○ Ensures customer team's consensus on the results

- <u>Desired Feedback</u>. Be specific about the feedback you expect from the customer. For example:

  - Program Focus. Do you agree with the stated focus and benefits of the program?

  - Benefits. Do the line items in the Value Model represent a complete, relevant list of quantifiable benefits (Pain Point – Value Statement pairs)? Is there any redundancy or potential double-counting of value? Are we missing any Benefits?

  - Driver and Financial Factors. For a given Benefit, are these the right metrics? Are there better ways to quantify the value of a given line item?

  - Improvement Factors. Are the impacts clearly explained through the factor naming? Is the level of improvement specified reasonable or should it be modified?

  - Situational Impacts. Are there specific situations that will impact the factor values being used? (e.g., wage rate variations by geographic location; event occurrence rates may vary by industry; or improvement factors may vary based on which portions of the solution are enabled)? Should these 'situational impacts' be reflected in the model?

  - Capabilities. Do you agree that the stated solution Capabilities for each Benefit deliver on the promise of the value statement?

  - Proof Points. Can you provide any anecdotes or empirical data from your experience that supports the value statement claim? As part of validation exercise, the baseline values in the data model should be 'hardened' with supporting customer data or industry benchmarks that they may have on hand. Ideally, the customer should provide values for the Driver, Improvement, and Financial Factors.

o   Are Value Categories in the model consistent with your critical success factors? Are there other preferred ways to group benefits in the model to reflect customer experience?

o   Assets. Are the assets generated relevant and supportive of the internal investment decision making process? What changes would you suggest?

ENABLE IT – Best Practices to Promote Adoption

With CVM program validation complete, you're now ready to enable the various stakeholders involved in customer delivery. The good news is that much of the content you need for enablement training has already been developed. It's largely a matter of repurposing and packaging this *know-how* to give the sales team members the confidence to carry on effective value conversations throughout the customer engagement process. In this way, enablement content will achieve the following organizational change goals:

- Raise awareness for the need to change. Why change? What's in it for me?

- Create a bias for action. Why now?

- Accredit or certify the skills required by sales reps to perform as a Trusted Advisor and first line Sales Managers as effective value coaches.

Thereafter, the enablement challenge is to continually *reinforce* behavior by recognizing and promoting success.

As a Value Practitioner your active participation in building and delivering enablement training provides an excellent opportunity to demonstrate leadership and promote your visibility and image as a key contributor to the success of the business.

So, let's see how this is done.

Package Enablement Training Content

Enablement content can be packaged and delivered in a variety of ways — including recorded sessions on a Learning Management System; formal face-to-face venues like sales roadshows, Sales Kick-off events, on-boarding events; and one-on-one coaching sessions. The table below suggests a way to repurpose and package the *know-how* that was already created as part of the Build It stage.

Figure 2.23. Repurposing Content for Enablement Training

Enablement Asset	Description
CVM Sales Playbook	For *internal-use-only*, provides CVM Program context, key concepts underlying the Value Data Model, sales team roles and responsibilities for the customer engagement process. References and links to the key sales assets previously developed; specifically: • CVM Elevator Pitch • Customer CVM Program Data Sheet Handout • FAQ documents: (1) Objection Handling and (2) Responses to Economic Buyer during presentation • Customer CVM Program Introductory briefing (PPT) • Value Statement Checklist and Discovery Questions • Business Case Presentation Template (PPT)
CVM Program Quick Reference Guide	For *internal-use-only*, a one-page summary of the CVM engagement process and sales assets
LMS Voice-over PPT: *Value Conversations that Matter*	Recorded training in the CVM engagement process and playbook – including how CVM aligns with the sales process, related sales frameworks like MEDDIC, Challenger, Miller Heiman, and your go-to-market strategy. Possibly used as prework for a major sales event (e.g., SKO).
LMS Voice-over PPT: *Language of Business Value Selling*	Recorded training introducing the metrics Economic Buyers use to make investment decisions (e.g., ROI, IRR, NPV, Payback, TCO) – along with the advantages and disadvantages of each metric. Possibly used as prework for a major sales event (e.g., SKO).

Enablement Asset	Description
Face-to-face PPT decks for sales events	Formal presentation used to introduce the CVM Program to sales teams at key sales events (e.g., SKO or roadshows); generate enthusiasm; explain rollout plan; and clarify expectations with a call to action
Case Study	A domain-specific customer case study used as prework for a role-play workshop at major sales event
Model Reference Catalogue	Fact sheet for each solution value model describing what and how to use the models — including a list of benefits, descriptions, factors used, and discovery questions to ask
Library of proposals / business cases	Perhaps redacted or organized by industry or solution type, the library describes what was done with a specific company to get the deal across the finish line. Ideally, this would be followed up with a value realization assessment showing what the customer actually achieved relative to the baseline ROI business case
Value Model Quick Reference Sheet	Standard Reference Document for sellers that shows the benefit category, name, benefit description and factors
Value Modelling 'Cheat' Sheet	Early sales cycle engagement cheat sheet with questions to help reps through early discovery process leading to meaningful mid stage conversation and get prospect buy-in to collaborate on a business case. Essentially empower sales reps to execute a 'deal desk' process: validate sales situation; determine initiatives; prioritize benefits.
Deal Success Stories	For *internal-use-only*, brief (1-2 page) write-ups highlighting deal successes attributable to the CVM-generated business case – featuring best practices, sales team testimonials, and key deal attributes (size, time to close, etc.)
White paper: *Economics of B2B Solution*	Customer-facing document describing the economics of a B2B solution along with an overview of the process and methodology that customers have used to quantify business value
Customer ROI Spotlights	One or two-page customer-facing write-ups documenting the business value a specific customer has realized implementing the B2B solution

Let's get back to our case study to see how CyberSecure used some of this content at their annual sales kick-off event to launch their CVM Program.

CASE STUDY EPISODE 4: Communicating What GREAT Looks Like at Sales Kick-off

John Cash asked Susan Smart and his management team to prepare for introducing the CyberValue Program at their annual Sales Kick-off Event. His guidance to Susan and his team:

- Generate enthusiasm for the CyberValue Program
- Explain the rollout plan
- Clarify expectations with a call to action

The team agreed that the sales teams should be given some pre-work assignments to prepare for the event. Specifically, the sales team was required to view and gain accreditation for two recorded courses.

- *Value Conversations that Matter.* Introduction to the CyberValue engagement process, value model, and sales playbook – including how the CyberValue Program aligns with the sales process, MEDDIC, and the go-to-market strategy.

- *Language of Business Value Selling.* Introduction to the metrics Economic Buyers use to make investment decisions (e.g., ROI, IRR, NPV, Payback, TCO) – along with the advantages and disadvantages of each metric.

In addition, the sales team was provided with a case study to be used as the basis for a role-playing workshop at the event.

The management team prepared the following agenda to connect the dots between the sales process, MEDDIC, and the CyberValue Program.

- Session 1. Sales Process Overview. An introduction to the prescribed sales process – prerequisites, desired outcomes, and best practices for each stage.

- Session 2. MEDDIC Overview.

- Session 3. Value Pyramid. A prescribed way for reps to document each deal based on their account research.

- Session 4. CyberValue Program Introduction – connecting the dots between the prescribed sales process and CyberValue

    o Formal presentation: *Selling Business Value – Here's What GREAT Looks like*

        ▪ Today's Buyer-Seller Challenges

        ▪ The Solution: What GREAT looks like

        ▪ How do we get there?

    o Workshop ('Let's do this together'). Using the case study pre-work assignment, teams of six individuals were given the following assignments related to the customer engagement process:

        ▪ Sell IT. How would you pitch the CyberValue Program to the Economic Buyer and Champion to gain agreement to collaborate with us on a business case? What objections do you expect to get? How would you overcome them?

        ▪ Frame IT. Select 4-5 Benefits from the CyberSecure solution value model that you feel would resonate with the Economic Buyer and Champion

    o Role Playing. Three teams (selected at random) present their results to a CyberSecure sales executive role playing the Economic Buyer.

    o Demonstration of CVM Platform. Using data provided in the case study, the CyberSecure value model and automation platform is used to demonstrate how the closing stages of the engagement process were completed; specifically, how to:

        ▪ Model / Refine It. Customize a value model for this deal

- **Present It.** Deliver and defend the business case and address Economic Buyer questions
  - o Call to Action. Following the demonstration, clarify expectations of the sales teams:
    - Complete online courses and Knowledge Assessment
    - Review reference materials
    - Gain confidence in participating in business value conversations
    - Sell It to buyers and customers
    - Report progress at deal reviews and QBRs

The approach worked like a charm. Following SKO, sales team members were chomping at the bit to get more detailed information and training.

Best Practices for Motivation and Enablement

As you package enablement content and deliver training, there are a number of other helpful principles and practices to keep in mind – geared to achieving the goals of motivation, know-how, and empowering all stakeholders to engage customers in meaningful conversations.

Focus on role-based enablement. Effective enablement should be geared to drive CVM adoption and usage. Work with the Sales Enablement / Sales Operation team to assess skills and needs for each stakeholder role / profile – e.g., Sales Account Managers, SDRs, Sales Support, Sales Management, Executive Management, Program Management, Value Experts, Customers. Develop the right level of training for different role / skill profiles – including on-boarding new sales team members.

Emphasis should be placed on the customer conversation;
this is even more important than generating numbers.

<u>Certify Sales Managers as effective mentors / coaches</u>. First line sales managers must serve as effective coaches and play a key role in managing demand. Value conversations should be built into all deal inspection reviews and QBRs – including discussion of the specific pain point – value statement pairs that are driving each opportunity.

<u>Stage the initial CVM rollout</u>. Initially, rollout the CVM program to a small group of key players to test and refine the enablement strategy. It's a good idea to have sales managers and a few key sales reps complete the training before full rollout. A few caveats:

- Do not rollout the CVM program until sales managers are ready to coach
- Successful usage of the CVM platform requires an appropriate level of formal training followed by hands-on usage and coaching. Do not allow users to access the CVM automation platform until formal training is completed as acumen must reach the right level before use of CVM automation will be effective. Don't assume that even people familiar with use of spreadsheets can jump directly into CVM automation without proper training and a hard reset on 'why we do it at all'
- Getting users to the right level of acumen will also help manage demand.

<u>Get the Customer Success team in the loop</u>. Customer Success stands to gain considerably by having a post implementation value realization assessment capability. Getting this team involved early on in defining the initial baseline business case helps set expectations and sets the stage for a comparison of actual value achieved versus the initial ROI baseline.

<u>Anticipate bumps in the road</u>. As with any organizational change, you will need to overcome inertia – the natural resistance to use something new and imperfect. For example, the initial value model may be missing benefits, fail to accommodate all sales situations, or contain inadequate benchmark data which may lead to unrealistic ROI projections. This is to be expected. But every journey begins with a single step. The value model and sales assets will continually improve as you gain more first-hand customer and sales team feedback. Remember, 'done is good.' An agile CVM approach means

reaching a minimally viable model early on and then refining it incrementally over time as you gain more direct field experience.

> **Always keep in mind Vince Lombardi's philosophy:**
> *"Perfection is not attainable.*
> *But if we chase perfection, we can catch excellence."*
> **Progress can be stymied if you allow perfection**
> **to be the enemy of 'good enough' to start with.**

Reinforcement: Locking in the Customer Value Management Culture

Enablement is not a one-time event. It requires continuous involvement of sales leadership, ongoing visibility, and reinforcement — keeping the CVM program front and center in everyone's minds. To this end, here are some helpful principles and practices to consider.

The **5W** Approach. One sales executive requires each member of the sales team to prove that their buyer Champion can answer five questions: **W**hy the initiative; **W**hy us; **W**hat is the expected business value; **W**hen; **W**hy now. Communicating this approach is reinforced by conducting Workshops and deal reviews with sales teams.

Encourage participation at Annual Sales Roadshows. Have sales team members deliver a 20-minute presentation sharing CVM best practice success stories (e.g., what Benefits and Assumptions resonate best with customers for a given solution). These presentations help sales teams understand (a) the specific value hypotheses that resonate with companies of a certain size and scale and (b) how CVM was used to determine the solution they should pitch.

Establish a continuous feedback loop. It's important to provide guidance to sales teams on 'what is' and 'is not' working. To this end:

- Routinely conduct a model usage assessment to help keep models fresh. How many and which benefits are most commonly used? Which benefits typically resonate and work well with customers? Which assumptions are most commonly altered?

- Explain ways to cross check work to ensure that value propositions are within parameters / thresholds that are successful. For example: *this is the level of ROI and payback period that appear to be credible.*

- Leverage a social media platform to exchange information on best practices.

<u>Be proactive about promoting success and measuring adoption</u>. Recognize that managers and sales reps typically will not volunteer success stories and lessons learned without reminders. Be proactive about capturing and sharing lessons learned and consider 'gamifying' adoption and use by rewarding early adopters, celebrating wins, and looking for ways to encourage those players reluctant to change.

Encourage managers to routinely get in the practice of sharing stories about how CVM helped close deals. To this end, establish a routine cadence of calls to keep the program front-and-center. Consider for example:

- *Weekly* Field Enablement calls to share usability 'tips and tricks' on how to successfully leverage CVM. Translate feedback into documented success stories to ensure that new reps are provided with important lessons learned. Continuous reinforcement (reminders) is also important — perhaps repeating some of the basics even as more advanced topics are introduced.

- *Biweekly* adoption sessions to ensure that everyone that should be using CVM is using assets at the right point in the sales cycle.

- *Monthly* sales meetings led by a sales leader to highlight success stories. Provide a PPT template to have sales reps highlight one or two opportunities that were closed in the previous month and how CVM worked. What assets were used? How did the conversation go? What was the impact on the sale? This practice has a number of benefits: provides visibility to sales leadership of program effectiveness;

provides recognition to individual sales reps; provides guidance to sales teams on what works well; leads to continuous positive reinforcement.

- Publish Deal Success Stories on the Internal Community Page. These internal-use only stories provide best practices to raise sales rep acumen. Recognize that people are at different stages in their ability to use CVM assets; thus, tips and tricks must be communicated accordingly.

MANAGE IT – Setup the Processes Required to Ensure Continuous Improvement

The 'Manage It' step closes the loop by measuring adoption and usage; promoting successes; and ensuring visibility and improvement of the CVM Program on an ongoing basis. While we plan to drill down in more detail into the steady state Manage-It stage in Part 4, it's important to think through the required processes and success measures up-front as part of the CVM Program launch.

As noted above, building and maintaining the content for the CVM program requires recognizing that there are multiple types and levels of content to consider (e.g., benefit calculation methodology, benefit meta data, sales asset output templates, and supporting material). The objectives and use case for each content type and a process for maintaining the freshness and relevance of all content should be clearly defined. To this end, there are a number of key processes that must be established and formalized.

<u>CVM Content Maintenance Management</u> ensures that standardized processes and procedures are used for all changes, facilitate efficient and prompt handling of all changes, and maintain the proper balance between the need for change and the potential detrimental impact of changes. Changes to value models come from a number of sources.

- Customers provide feedback on the relative importance and relevance of benefits in the models which may lead to adding or deleting benefits, updating improvement factors, revising situations, or changing assumptions in the baseline model

- Value Realization assessments provide empirical data that affects the various factors in the baseline value model or contribute to case study and proof points that should be added

- New products (created internally or as the result of acquisitions) may require new value models or changes to existing models to accommodate new capabilities and features

- Software upgrades to the CVM Automation platform.

Problem Management. A sister discipline of CVM Content Maintenance Management, Problem Management aims to resolve the root causes of issues that may arise from poor infrastructure performance, deficiencies in the value models, or inadequate user training. Whatever the cause, these issues should be resolved in a way that satisfies end user expectations for responsiveness and prevents problem recurrence.

Release Management involves planning the rollout of CVM software and value model updates; effectively communicating and managing expectations of the customer during the planning and rollout of new software or model releases; and controlling the distribution and installation of changes.

Demand Management takes a number of forms.

- External. Supporting the field in customer engagements

The good news: an agile CVM automation platform provides the ability to support 100% of qualified deals.

- Internal. Managing stakeholder expectations for enhancements to the CVM Program; for example:

  o Marketing may be interested in collecting first-hand customer experience information for case study material and marketing collateral.

  o Product Management will be interested in feedback from customers to help understand the value of specific product capabilities or new requirements that drive product roadmaps.

  o Customer Success will likely want to be involved in setting buyer expectations in the initial business case, because it provides an important baseline for measuring post-implementation customer satisfaction.

Security Management. Because Value Models are designed to differentiate your value from competitors, they represent a form of IP that must be protected. As explained above, this is another important consideration in the selection of your CVM automation platform. It's also the reason why a central repository of value models, representing a single source of truth, lends itself to a more secure environment than spreadsheets owned by individuals who would take their knowledge with them should they leave the company.

This completes our discussion of how to launch an enterprise-scale CVM Program. Now we are ready to move on to describe how the content and infrastructure described herein is used to engage prospective buyers and current customers in meaningful value conversations.

PART 3
CUSTOMER ENGAGEMENT:
MANAGING CVM DELIVERY

PART 3: Customer Engagement: Managing CVM Delivery

CVM Delivery Goal: Create the GREAT Buyer-seller Experience

The primary goal of CVM Delivery is to provide first-hand evidence that the use of the CVM automation platform and repository of content developed during the CVM Launch Stage results in meaningful value conversations throughout the customer engagement cycle. In short, that transformation to a value-centric sales model 'moves the needle' toward a GREAT buyer-seller experience.

Once again, we return to our organizational change model for guidance on goals, specifically:

- How do we *motivate* potential buyers and customers to collaborate with us on a business case?
- What *know-how* is required on the part of customers to make this happen?
- How do we *reinforce* this behavior to make the change stick?

Addressing these issues requires engaging different buyer personas to agree that quantifying their value to the business is critical to their success. They need to know how to quantify the business value of the investment in tools they need to get their job done. And they need to quantify and showcase the business value of their current investments on a continuing basis.

CVM Delivery Success Measures

The focus of CVM Delivery is to engage <u>prospective buyers</u> and <u>existing customers</u> in meaningful value conversations – helping you gain credibility as a Trusted Advisor. With prospective buyers these conversations should lead to Economic Buyer ownership of a defensible business case. With existing customers, the goal is to quantify and showcase value realized, lock in renewals and open the door to cross-sell and upsell opportunities.

To this end (as illustrated below), the CVM data model developed as part of the Launch Stage supports two distinct but related use cases.

- Use Case 1 is to build a business case that also serves as the ROI Baseline from which future progress is measured. This requires an analysis of a customer's current state relative to a desired future state.

- Use Case 2 uses the ROI baseline model created in Use Case 1 to measure and showcase value realized.

Figure 3.1: CVM Data Model Use Cases: (1) Building a Business Case and (2) Showcasing Value Realized

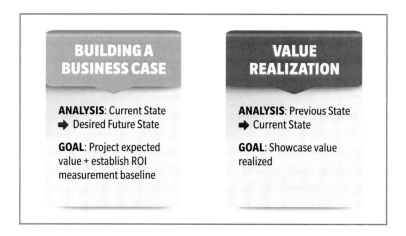

Evidence of completing this stage is a function of the satisfaction of your two key stakeholder communities. Thus, success measures for this stage might include the following.

External Stakeholders (Prospective Buyers and Existing Customers)	Internal (Sales team; sales enablement; marketing; customer success)
• Prospective buyers. Willingness to collaborate on and accept ownership of business case • Existing Customers. Customer satisfaction as evidenced by renewals, expanded use of a solution, ROI case studies, testimonials, and references	• More deals • Bigger deals • Faster deals • Improved Net Revenue Retention • Success Stories

Delivery Challenges

Achieving these outcomes requires recognizing and addressing a number of related buyer-seller challenges as outlined in the table below.

Figure 3.2: Value Delivery Challenges for Sellers and Buyers

Buyer Challenges / Concerns	Seller Implications / Challenges
Buyer skepticism. Buyers are understandably leery of a seller-provided business case and ROI projection. Overly-simplistic calculators that lead to claims of 1000% ROI with 4-month payback are unreal and impeach credibility.	Gaining customer buy-in to collaborate. To overcome buyer skepticism and establish credibility as a Trusted Advisor, sales reps need a credible end-to-end quantification process and methodology. In particular, CVM must deliver a rigorous, transparent approach from business case development through value realization measurement. Essentially, the ROI model used to close the deal, should also be used as the baseline against which value achieved post implementation is measured.

Buyer Challenges / Concerns	Seller Implications / Challenges
Limited time to engage sales people. Economic buyers have little time to engage directly with sales people – especially when a sales person leads with a product pitch. They typically direct the sales person down the organization to a less senior technical manager, who may influence but does not make the decision to buy.	Effective way to reach / gain attention of the Economic Buyer & Champion. Sales reps need confidence and sufficient financial acumen to engage in meaningful business value conversations. Failure to have a business value conversation often leads to discounting that erodes quota attainment. A 'pricing war' is impossible to win without the right ammunition. Perhaps worse, without a compelling financial justification for change, sales reps risk losing to the status quo or the "no decision" outcome.
Getting internal stakeholder consensus on investment decisions. Economic Buyers typically want to get their entire team on board to justify an investment that has enterprise-wide implications. Orchestrating this 'buy-in' in a systematic way is challenging.	Efficient engagement process. Facilitate a non-intrusive process that features reusable templates for capturing and assimilating data into a fully traceable business case that can be iteratively refined as the buyer takes ownership of the metrics and the message. Content at the right altitude for different buyer personas. Since multiple decision influencers are involved in the buying decision, content must be packaged and communicated for each level of the buyer organization.
No budget for a new tool. Annual budgets are already locked. A new requirement for a solution therefore requires reallocating budgeted funds – often a stiff obstacle to overcome.	Answering the 3 key questions: Why Buy? Why Now? Why from you? What specific problem is addressed? What's the compelling event? How does your business value stack up against other funding alternatives (e.g., alternative uses of capital; direct competitors; the dreaded 'No Decision' option)? Number of solutions to sell. Solution providers may have multiple solutions to sell. Thus, the quantification methodology must provide a flexible, understandable way to project ROI across a variety of solution 'combinations' without double-counting value.

Buyer Challenges / Concerns	Seller Implications / Challenges
Measuring and showcasing value realized to continue investing in the existing solution and also to help justify expanded implementation. Existing customers may intuitively recognize the value of a limited implementation of a B2B solution and want to expand its use to other parts of the organization, but cannot because they lack the ability to measure and showcase the value realized from current investments.	Guarantee renewal by proving the value achieved in the previous cycle of investment. Cross-selling / upselling solutions in existing accounts becomes a significant challenge when the business value of current investments cannot be measured. Reps need a way to measure value realized to help justify renewals and expand the solution footprint.
End User Adoption. How can we be assured that end users will take advantage of the solution? How can we overcome expected organizational inertia to change?	Effective Role-based Enablement. Reps must be prepared to recommend a proven CVM rollout approach that targets all end user roles. Importantly, first line sales managers must be accredited as effective value coaches. Continuous Improvement. Set the expectation that the initial baseline value model, while serving as a helpful strawman, will evolve over time as more customer experience leads to improvement.

Guiding Principles and Framework for CVM Delivery

To address these challenges and achieve success, the figure below highlights the five key steps associated with selling and delivering CVM to customers – explained as follows.

1. **SELL IT** addresses the need to *motivate* action on the part of the Economic Buyer and Champion.

2. **FRAME IT** involves agreeing with the buyer on the subset of benefits from the solution value model that will be used in the business case. The buyer must be ready, willing, and able to provide the data and assumptions needed to refine the value hypothesis.

3. **REFINE IT** is the iterative process of working with the buyer's team to refine the business case – using data and assumptions to override the default values in the value model.

4. **PRESENT IT** involves co-presenting the results of the modeling exercise to the Economic Buyer. The goal: transfer ownership of the business case from the seller to the buyer.

5. ***MEASURE IT*** requires the periodic assessment of the value realized as compared to the initial ROI baseline model.

Figure 3.3: Framework for CVM Customer Engagement

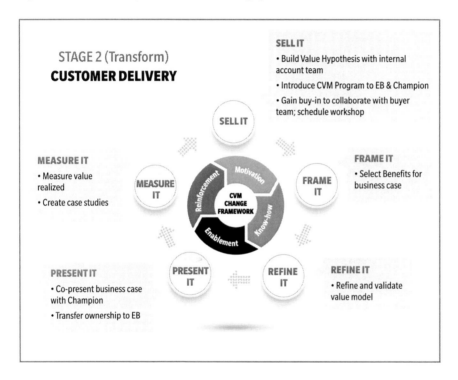

Not surprisingly, this framework looks similar to the Launch Framework described in Part 2. Recall that the launch framework begins with selling the value of the CVM program to your <u>internal</u> stakeholders. In the CVM delivery framework, we begin by selling the value of collaboration to the <u>external</u> buyer or customer. Let's elaborate on each step in this framework before we dive back into the case study to further clarify how this works in practice.

Sell It – Getting Buy-in to Collaborate

The **Sell It** stage is all about raising customer awareness to the existence of the CVM program and gaining agreement to collaborate. It addresses the 'what's-in-it-for-me' question – helping the customer understand the personal value of collaboration and reinforcing your credibility as a Trusted Advisor. To this end, there are a number of steps to take.

1. Do your homework by properly researching the account

2. Package your knowledge in a way that demonstrates your understanding of the customer's business challenges and potential business value of your solution. The use of a 'Value Pyramid' (described subsequently) is a proven approach.

3. Introduce the CVM Program to the Economic Buyer and Champion -- providing a value hypothesis, addressing questions and concerns, explaining how the process works, expected customer commitment and timetable and gaining buy-in to collaborate on a refined business case.

Once you gain commitment to collaborate, you're ready to move on to the other steps in the process – beginning with selecting the benefits that resonate with the customer, and for which they are comfortable providing data and assumption. This brings us to the Frame It step.

Frame It – Selecting Benefits for the Baseline Business Case

Recall that the baseline value model contains the 'universe' of benefits associated with your solution. Not all benefits are applicable to every customer. So, it's important to get agreement on the subset of benefits that are relevant for each opportunity.

There are two ways to go about this.

1. As noted above, as part of the Sell It stage, you can work with your account team to build a strawman value hypothesis as a way of engaging the customer. Presenting this strawman would then be part of the formal CVM introduction to the customer.

2. Alternatively, you can work with your customer Champion to select the subset of benefits (a) that resonate and (b) for which they are ready to revise and support. As part of this conversation, you should strive to agree on the top 3- 5 priorities (*'what problems / pain are you dealing with'*) and the supporting benefits to be quantified in the business case to address this pain. The total number of benefits will vary based on the scope and complexity of the solution; however, keep in mind that it is difficult to comprehend and get agreement on more than 10 – 12 benefits in total. Using the CVM platform to do this will improve the experience for both the buyer and the sales team over time as it is more interactive and results in better buy-in to the process and results -- replacing the more traditional exchange of documents via email (*'we give you a document to complete; you send it back.'*).

Once benefits are selected and a strawman model is created, you have the structure for a more formal workshop to refine the model and create a defensible business case.

Refine It – Refining a Bullet-proof Business Case

Customization of a business case for a specific buyer should be a matter of refining the initial strawman Value Hypothesis. In fact, using your Value Hypothesis as a starting point you can use the CVM process to structure the refinement conversation as follows.

1. Specify the sales situation -- including the targeted account; relevant solution(s) involved; industry and geography considerations that may affect baseline data values; scaling parameters; and other variables that drive the ROI calculation (e.g., discount rate).

2. Review Benefits. Make sure the buyer team agrees on the appropriate groupings and specific benefits that will be included in the model.

3. Provide numbers. Examine all the assumptions in the model and override the default values with customer-provided data.

4. Add Costs. The calculation of ROI, payback and other investment metrics require adding costs into the model. Costs should include software license / subscriptions costs, infrastructure, people, and services over the project life.

5. Review Results. The CVM platform should do the rest – calculating key investment metrics (e.g., ROI, Payback Period, NPV, and the 3-month cost of delay and providing a number of displays such as distribution of value; year-by-year Cost-Benefit analysis; and a cash flow table.

The model refinement process is typically iterative. The CVM platform provides 'levers' to allow the buyer team to ratchet assumptions up or down to quickly see how sensitive the ROI calculation is to different assumptions. These levers include:

- Turning benefits 'on' or 'off' (considered 'soft' or not included at all) in the model

- Editing key inputs such as driver and financial factors

- Modifying expected impacts and improvements

- Benefit realization percent. How quickly will a given benefit be realized?

- Choosing currency and language for the customer presentation

The result of the business case refinement exercise should be buyer team consensus on the final business case – benefits, ROI, payback period, etc. Once that goal is achieved, you're ready to package the results for presentation to the Economic Buyer.

Present It – Co-presenting the Business Case and Transferring Ownership

The final step in the process is Present It. This of course is where the 'rubber meets the road' – packaging and delivering the buyer team's consensus on a business case to the Economic Buyer, defending it, and addressing any remaining issues. The goal is to transfer ownership of the business case from the seller to the buyer.

1. As a best practice, it's a good idea to begin by coaching and empowering your Champion to defend the business case. While it's important that the you're fully prepared to do this, it's perhaps even more important that your Champion is prepared to take the business case forward to justify the investment. After all, you may not be in the room when the business case is discussed.

Getting approval for the investment does not represent the end of the journey; in fact, it is just the beginning of the customer value journey. The business case creates the framework for scoping and implementation decisions and serves as a guideline to help ensure that the project team remains focused on the anticipated business outcomes of the solution. After implementation, the journey continues by using the baseline business case to measure value realized — making necessary adjustments along the way to achieve expected results and capture actual value achieved.

Measure It: Collaborating to Measure and Report Value Realized

Many times, a customer focuses on using the value model as the justification to get funding, then shelves it absent a credible way to use it as the baseline to measure value realized. As noted above, the value model has a use case beyond initially justifying the deal.

The Measure It stage closes the loop on the customer value management chain – driving continuous improvement of both the customer engagement process and the underlying value model and associated sales assets.

While the initial business case sets customer expectations relative to expected business value, an effective CVM process also includes (a) an ability to quantify the actual value realized versus the planned ROI baseline model following implementation of the solution; (b) a prescriptive mechanism for making adjustments to enable further value realization; (c) a way to capture testimonials, case studies and 'proof points' based on actual customer results; and (d) recommended improvements to the solution and the core Solution Value Model(s).

As suggested in the table below, the value measurement process involves a variety of roles with different expectations. Note that 'Customer Contact(s)' typically include the Economic Buyer, Champion, or other representative from the customer that is monitoring adoption and effectiveness of the implemented solution.

Figure 3.4: Value Measurement Roles and Responsibilities

Attribute	Customer Success Manager (Seller)	Value Practitioner (Seller)	Customer Contact(s) (Buyer)
Role	• Initiate Value Realization exercise with Customer • Review / Present Results • Remedial Action as required • Track Value Realization exercises by Region, Rep, Account	• Conduct Value Realization exercise / survey and process results • Co-present results and identify opportunities to drive additional / incremental value from the B2B solution based on the Value Realization analysis	• Responsible for Solution Implementation and Value Realization from a customer point of view
Interests	• How is customer progressing relative to projected ROI? • Which value statements are on target? Which are at risk? • What corrective actions need to be taken to achieve goal? • Are there proof points, testimonials and customer success stories that can be	• Are we achieving targeted business value for each value statement in customer business case? • How do we improve the quality and usefulness of the value map(s)? • How do we incorporate the insights and proof points garnered from	• Are we achieving our expected outcomes? • What adjustments are required to achieve expected outcomes? • Have we identified opportunities to drive additional / incremental

Attribute	Customer Success Manager (Seller)	Value Practitioner (Seller)	Customer Contact(s) (Buyer)
	gathered for incorporation in future value analyses	customer interactions	value from the B2B solution?
Business outcomes	• Efficient delivery of Value Realization service • Customer satisfaction • Renewals • Cross sell / Upsell	• Customer Satisfaction • Continuous improvement of Product and Value Model(s)	• Proof that investment met expectations
Outputs	• Value Realization results • Case studies, library of customer success stories, proof points, testimonials	• Value Realization Survey Templates • Case Study templates • Solution & Value Map Improvements	• Value Realization results • Case Studies / proof points inputs

That's sufficient grounding in the customer engagement framework, principles, and practices. Now let's return to our CyberSecure Case Study to see how Peter and Susan engaged the executive team at the ABC Financial Services Company account to achieve the goals in our delivery framework.

CASE STUDY EPISODE 5: Researching CyberSecure's Opportunity at ABC Financial Services

Peter Sellers, CyberSecure Sales Account Executive, is excited by what he learned at the recent sales kick-off event. He sees a potential opportunity to introduce the approach to one of his accounts – ABC Financial Services Company. He calls Susan Smart, CyberSecure Value Practitioner, and explains the buyer situation to her as follows.

Harry Ross, CIO of the ABC Financial Services Company, is deeply disturbed. Two months ago, at a QBR with the CEO, the subject of cybersecurity came up. The CEO and CFO were alarmed by recent headlines about the impact of malware attacks, email vulnerabilities, and crippling ransomware incidents.

In one incident, Acme Diagnostics disclosed that a potential breach of the billings collections system via a watering hole attack exposed sensitive data of 1.9 million patients. The exposed data included medical information, financial information such as credit card numbers and bank account information, and other personal information like Social Security numbers – exposing Acme to regulatory non-compliance penalties, significant customer notification costs, and brand damage.

When asked by the CEO how vulnerable ABC Financial Services was to cybersecurity threats, Harry realized he needed to have a clearer picture of their vulnerabilities and a plan of action. He immediately authorized a security audit. He was rattled by the result.

Auditors identified a number of issues that needed prompt attention, including:

1. 60% of their malware infections were due to phishing attacks and web-based watering hole attacks. Their Security Engineering team was spending 500 hours / month on malware containment.

2. The investments Harry had made in traditional perimeter detect-and-respond solutions (Firewalls, Anti-Virus and IDS/IPS) were not identifying and stopping advanced malware attacks (both via email and web). As a result, a staff of 4 people on their IT team was allocated to reimaging and restoring systems every week.

3. Moreover, denying uncategorized sites created an overwhelming number of recategorization requests to the Help Desk. The number of tickets to re-categorize per day was approximately 2000 across 10,000 employees. Greater than 75% of these requests were non-work related such as veterinarian research, schools, soccer little league, etc. It was taking 5 dedicated people to parse through and handle the requests.

In addition, ABC Financial has implemented a number of costly secure web gateways (SWGs) and integrated AV/Sandbox solutions – spending $300,000 each year. Harry wants to know if this is the best use of his budget. He asked his CSO, Mildred Pierce, to respond to the audit with recommendations and a plan.

Fortunately for Mildred she was already engaged in discussions with Peter Sellers from CyberSecure. Mildred needed help. While she had seen a demo and intuitively recognized the merits of CyberSecure solutions, she needed to provide Harry with a credible business case and plan.

Peter has never met Harry. Mildred warns: *'Harry is a tough guy to reach. He's definitely not interested in a product pitch and is leery of sales reps that use overly simplistic calculators to come up with ludicrous ROI projections.'* She asks for Peter's advice on how to proceed.

In the pages that follow, we will trace the journey of these key players, given what we already know about the status of the CyberSecure CVM program rollout.

CASE STUDY EPISODE 6: Packaging Account Research as a Value Pyramid

Once Peter learned about the ABC Financial Services situation from Mildred Pierce (CSO), he and Susan immediately got to work. Peter had already compiled a good bit of research on ABC Financial Services from the ABC company website, Annual Report, LinkedIn, and publicly available financial information.

He knew that using a Value Pyramid to package this information would demonstrate that he had done his homework and would prepare him for the '3-Whys' conversation with Harry and Mildred: Why Buy; Why Now; Why from CyberSecure.

Figure 3.5: Value Pyramid for ABC Financial Service

BUSINESS OBJECTIVES
- Maintain 10% + YOY Rev Growth
- Expand Market Share
- Grow valuation to maximize IPO position at right time

BUSINESS STRATEGIES
- Invest capital from funding round to accelerate revenue growth
- Invest in Innovation (cybersecurity)
- Attract Top Tier Talent to accelerate growth
- Capitalize on leadership position

BUSINESS INITIATIVES
- Secure Cloud Transformation
- Six Sigma / Lean Principles
- Talent: Attracting best & brightest
- Partner Growth

RISKS & CRITICAL CAPABILITIES
- Cost and risk associated with cloud transformation; risky end user behavior
- Endpoint device proliferation
- Increasing and evolving threat vectors
- Inadequate and costly traditional approaches to detect and respond
- Cybersecurity workforce constraints

CYBERSECURE SOLUTIONS

✓ CyberSecure prevents active web content from reaching the end-point; thus, all web sites present zero risk as malware infection from web links is virtually impossible,

✓ CyberSecure's SWG-powered Isolation provides completely secure internet access without the need to back-haul web traffic to central locations for security controls.

✓ CyberSecure's cloud-based solution reduces resources required to manage traditional on-premise SWG appliances by providing single policy administration

$2.3M
Potential Benefit (3 years)

Peter knew that while the number of layers in the pyramid are subjective, the content for ABC Financial Services should include:

- **Buyer Objectives.** *What are the buyer's business objectives?*

- **Business Strategies.** *What does the buyer intend to do to achieve their objectives?*

- **Business Initiatives.** *What specific initiatives does the buyer have in place to support their strategies?*

- **Risks & Critical Capabilities.** *What internal and external challenges / risks does the buyer face that could hinder the success of their initiatives?*

- **Solution capabilities.** *What solution capabilities will help the buyer address the risks / challenges and achieve their initiatives?*

In addition to the Value Pyramid, Peter and Susan wanted to structure the conversation with Harry and Mildred around a Value Hypothesis by packaging their account knowledge into a provocative, directional projection of the potential business value of the CyberSecure solution to ABC Financial Services.

CASE STUDY EPISODE 7: Creating a Value Hypothesis with the CyberSecure Account Team

In addition to the Value Pyramid, Peter and Susan decided to use the CyberValue automation platform to create a Value Hypothesis. They knew that the underlying value model would provide the structure required to consolidate the CyberSecure account team's knowledge of the ABC Financial Services opportunity. The resulting strawman value hypothesis would then be used to (a) establish credibility with Mildred and Harry Ross and (b) serve as the basis for further refinement with the ABC Financial Services management team.

To begin, Peter arranged a meeting with the internal CyberSecure account team. While Peter and team had little first-hand knowledge of ABC company financial data, team members did have some experience with other financial services customers. What information they did not have on hand, would be filled in by the industry benchmark data in the model. This combination of account and benchmark data would provide the coarse 'directional' sense of CyberSecure value needed to start the conversation with Mildred.

Peter outlined the process of customizing a value model for the ABC Financial Services Company as illustrated and described below. He clarified that this is an iterative process that would be first used by the account team to build the strawman and then again with the customer until Mildred and Harry accepted ownership of a defensible business case.

Figure 3.6: Using the CyberSecure Value Model to Build a Value Hypothesis

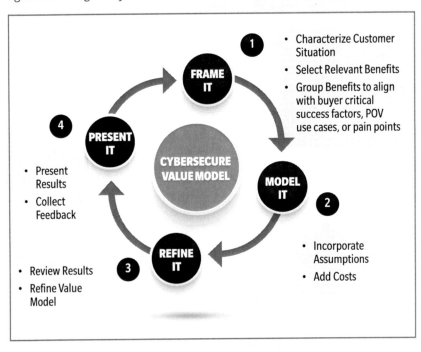

1. **Frame It**. First, using the CyberValue Automation Platform, Peter configured the Value Hypothesis specifically for the ABC Financial Services opportunity. He created a record for the account, selected the appropriate value model from the CyberValue library, and began to override default values in the model with the account team's input. This included:

    a. Specifying industry and geography. Configuring the model for a financial services company in the Americas region.

    b. Selecting use cases appropriate to ABC Financial Services requirements (e.g., stopping advanced malware attacks via both email and web).

    c. Sizing the model by specifying the approximate number of employees that would use the CyberSecure solution.

The baseline CyberValue data model was already populated with data for a number of other variables that are required to prepare a business case (such as cost of capital, term of deal, expected deployment time). Lacking insight into ABC's specific information, Peter decided to leave these default values in the model as placeholders for the time being.

To complete the framing exercise, Peter and team selected the specific benefits in the model that would resonate with Mildred and Harry. The baseline CyberValue Model had about 20 specific benefits to choose from. Keeping in mind that this was only a starting point for the conversation with Mildred, Peter elected to use the following subset of benefits from the model – helping him emphasize to Mildred that the model provided ABC Financial Services with the flexibility to quantify both <u>direct</u> (tangible) and <u>indirect</u> (soft) benefits.

Direct (Hard) Benefits	Indirect (Soft) Benefits
• Reduce Alert Analysis Cost • Reduce Malware Remediation Cost • Reduce Phishing Remediation Cost • Reduce Network Cost	• Protect Revenue Loss Due to Infections • Mitigate Destructive Attack / Extortion Risk • Mitigate Risk of End User Productivity Loss Due to Email and Web-based Attacks

To promote understanding and relevance to different ABC Financial Services stakeholders, Peter organized benefits into three logical categories:

- Business Critical Success Factors would appeal to executives and financial stakeholders. For ABC Financial Services, five value categories appeared to make sense: Security Operations Center Efficiency, IT Staff Efficiency, End User Efficiency, IT Asset Efficiency, and Business Risk Mitigation.

- Pain Points would clarify how benefits aligned with recognized business challenges. The following pain points were relevant to ABC Financial Services: Cybersecurity Workforce Shortage / Fatigue, High Network Backhaul Costs, Total Cost of Ownership of On-premise SWG Appliances, Continuously Evolving Threat Vectors.

- Proof of Value Use Cases would appeal to both sales and sales engineers and help connect the dots with technical due diligence requirements. Peter felt that Email Security and Web Security use cases would get the point across.

2. **Model It**. After selecting the relevant benefits, Peter moved on to building the initial value hypothesis. This required entering a few high-level inputs to calculate the financial value of each benefit. Peter is not a value professional, so he needs a straightforward, automated process to do this. Thankfully, the CyberValue platform provided a starter set of key assumptions already tailored to the size and specifics

of his selling situation – along with guidance on the "typical" range of values for him to adjust.

Peter has confidence that the default values are close enough for his initial hypothesis and elects to leave them as-is for now. He also knows that the calculation of ROI and other investment metrics that Mildred and Harry want to see require adding costs into the model. Because it is early in the process, Peter likely will not expose the costs to Mildred and Harry; however, by including cost estimates in the hypothesis he can generate meaningful investment metrics — ensuring that costs and benefits are in balance early in the conversation. He also includes any internal investment required by the customer to enable this solution, such as additional headcount or equipment to purchase.

Because the CyberValue model was prepopulated with benchmark data, Peter was not particularly concerned that he did not have every piece of ABC data on hand. He was comfortable that Mildred and Harry would understand that the value hypothesis was directional in nature and that he was simply trying to communicate how the collaboration process worked.

3. **Refine It**. After validating the initial benefits to include, refining key assumptions and providing costs, the CyberValue platform presents Peter with a summary of the investment metrics that can be used in his conversations with Mildred and Harry. As a reality check, he reviews a number of outputs automatically generated by the CyberValue automation platform – specifically:

   - Key investment metrics. Are the ROI, Payback Period, NPV, and the 3-month cost of delay reasonable? Are these values within the thresholds set as guidelines in the model? Peter is pleased that the automation platform provides explanations and formulas simply by clicking each metric.

- Distribution of value. Is the percent of value attributable to each value category realistic?

- Does the year-by-year Cost-Benefit analysis illustration help answer the question 'why buy now?'

This content helps Peter confidently prepare for discussions to socialize the numbers with Mildred and Harry.

After viewing these results, Peter meets with the account team to do further fine-tuning of the model. This is a helpful exercise, because Peter knows that this same 'refinement' process will be executed with the ABC Financial Services team once he gains agreement to collaborate.

4. **Present It**. Satisfied with the results of the exercise, Peter downloads a high level one-page summary (illustrated below) to introduce the potential value of CyberSecure for ABC Financial Services and get Harry's buy-in to engage in further value conversations.

Figure 3.7: CyberSecure Value Hypothesis

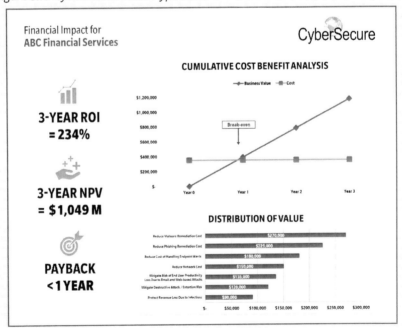

With a Value Pyramid and Value Hypothesis in hand, Peter and Susan are ready to meet Harry Ross.

CASE STUDY EPISODE 8: A Testy CIO asks: 'How Do You Calculate Your ROI Numerator?'

After Mildred's warning that Harry Ross (ABC Financial Services CIO) was sceptical about engaging with sellers to build a business case, Peter arranged a briefing to introduce the CyberValue Program to Mildred and Harry and get buy-in to collaborate on a business case. To prepare, Peter studied the enablement training content created by Susan:

- Elevator Pitch. Major points to make when introducing the CyberValue Program to a buyer

- FAQ 1: Objection Handling. Suggested responses to typical buyer questions who may be sceptical about collaborating with CyberSecure on a business case

- Customer CyberValue Program Introductory briefing (PPT). Used to introduce buyer's team to the CyberValue Program

- Customer Data Sheet Handout. One-page handout for customer providing an overview of the CyberValue Program — how it works and benefits to customer.

He felt well-prepared for his first meeting with Harry. Here's the substance of the dialogue between Peter and Harry following their exchange of pleasantries.

Peter: Mildred briefed me on the results of your recent audit and your urgency and interest in responding with the right solution. We recently introduced a Customer CyberValue program to respond to customers requesting our assistance in quantifying and showcasing the business value of CyberSecure solutions. It's a collaborative approach that is designed to make sure our solutions are a good fit for your requirements and that your investment can be justified based on the value to your business. It applies a proven methodology with minimal impact on your time and resources that will help gain your team's consensus on a business case with total transparency of results.

Harry: Yes Peter, Mildred mentioned the program to me. Perhaps she also explained that I've been down this road before with other vendors, only to be disappointed with the results. So, I'm more than a bit sceptical. Here's my concern: How do I know that the numbers you come up with are not skewed to your solution?

Peter: I can appreciate your concern. First, let me underscore that the program was launched initially to respond to existing customers who specifically asked for our assistance in justifying investments and showcasing value realized post implementation. This led to a rigorous and customer verified data model of value statements and an associated quantification approach that our customers (including your peers) found relevant and helpful. This same data model can be used to project potential business value to justify investments. Second, perhaps most importantly, you can include your specific data and assumptions in the model – overriding any and all default values (including industry benchmarks) that exist. The result is a business case that is transparent, you own, and is completely defensible.

Harry (deciding to test Peter by throwing a curve ball). Really. So, tell me how do you quantify the numerator in your ROI?

Peter. I'm pleased you asked because this highlights what I mean by transparency. The 'Net Benefits' part of our ROI (or what you refer to as the numerator) is certainly the toughest piece of the ROI equation to calculate. While the cost part is straightforward, the benefit side of the equation requires a credible methodology. Our approach is to embed the results of our customer experience in a value data model that provides full traceability of the ROI calculation down to the individual benefits that, when aggregated together for your situation, provide the basis for the Net Benefit calculation. Each Benefit in the model consists of a specific 'pain point – value statement' pair. You would only include the relevant benefits for which you're comfortable providing data and assumptions. Each selected Benefit is quantified by a straightforward 3-prong formula – driver factor, financial factor, and improvement factor. So, when your CFO asks 'where did this ROI percentage come from' you can show the full collection of benefits that comprise the ROI numerator.

Harry: Sounds interesting. I would be interested in seeing something that reflects the knowledge of my peers and relevant industry benchmarks. But (turning to Mildred), we should probably do a Proof of Concept first.

Peter: We would be pleased to work with you on a POC. However, we understand that proving that technology works is only one part of the due diligence process. Many of your peers have found that it is most efficient and productive to link your technical due diligence and business due diligence processes together – in fact, doing them in parallel. This essentially turns a Proof of Concept (POC) into a Proof of Value (POV).

Here's what we've seen as best practice. First, it is essential to gain your team's consensus on the Pain Points and Value Statements that drive the investment decision. Will the investment contribute to cost reduction, productivity gains, revenue growth, or risk mitigation? If so, in what way and how will these business outcomes be measured?

With this framework in hand, you can align the technical objectives of the POV with the business value statements to ensure you are testing these hypotheses and gathering appropriate empirical data to help populate your business case model (and override as many of the default values as possible). I understand you have an urgency to respond to the audit and get back to your CEO with a plan. This approach compresses the time it takes to complete the decision-making process and ensures that the underlying data and assumptions in the model are as realistic as possible. After all, what good is proving technical feasibility if the business value of technical capabilities is not clear?

Harry. What kind of a time commitment are you looking for from my team?

Peter. We're certainly sensitive to that issue. This is why we've taken steps to make our process as non-intrusive as possible. We've also implemented a value automation platform. Our team of seasoned professionals provides the data collection templates and facilitates the process. Your team provides the data that you have on hand, adjusts the assumptions in the model as appropriate, and socializes the results. This can be accomplished in a few email exchanges and a few short review sessions. It should not take more than one or two hours of your time. More than happy to walk your team through the process and clarify the time commitments required.

Harry. OK. That makes sense. I'd like to get the full management team's buy-in before proceeding. Mildred, please set up a 30-minute call with our team for Peter to more formally present the approach and clarify expectations.

CASE STUDY EPISODE 9: Formally Introducing Your CVM Process to the Buyer's Team

Mildred set up the presentation for the following week. In addition to setting the stage as he did with Harry, here's an outline of the formal presentation that Peter and Susan used.

Value Pyramid. First, to show that he had done his homework, Peter anchored his understanding of the ABC Financial Services situation the Value Pyramid slide illustrated and described earlier.

CyberValue Program Objectives. Next, Peter outlined the objectives of the program -- emphasizing the program is intended to be an "agile" collaboration between CyberSecure and ABC Financial Services with focus on:

a. quantifying the expected business value of investing in CyberSecure solutions;
b. aligning with the ABC Financial Services investment justification process; and
c. establishing a baseline to measure the value realized by ABC Financial Services after implementation.

Program Overview. Then, Peter showed how the baseline CyberSecure Value Model provides a framework for sharing knowledge gained from customers similar to ABC Financial Services and how this value model is surrounded by an efficient repeatable process (Frame It – Model It – Refine It – Present It).

Minimal Effort Required. Peter also explained how the program is designed to minimize disruption to ABC Financial Services as indicated in this table.

Figure 3.8: Communicating Value Modeling Resource Commitment to Buyer

Step	Activities	ABC Financial Services Resources	Staff Hours	Time Table
FRAME IT	CyberSecure facilitates kick-off workshop and presents process to customer team ABC Financial Services Team select relevant *Benefits*	ABC Financial Services Team	2-3 hour working session	Day 1: 2-3 hour working session
MODEL IT	CyberSecure builds strawman model with placeholder data and assumptions	NA	NA	Week 1
REFINE IT	ABC Financial Services overrides placeholder values in model with their data	ABC Financial Services Team	8 staff-hours	Week 2
PRESENT IT	CyberSecure packages and co-presents results	ABC Financial Services Team	2-hour session * # Team Members	Week 3

CyberValue Demonstration. Susan used the CyberValue automation platform to help highlight each step in the process as follows:

- **Frame It**. How the ABC Financial Services team selects the relevant Direct and Indirect benefits to be used in their model -- and for which they are comfortable providing data and assumptions (or agreeable to using the industry benchmarks provided as default values).

- **Model It**. Shows the specific elements that constitute a Benefit.

- **Refine It**. Explains the various 'levers' in the model that are used to override default values with ABC data and experience and ratchet down the results to arrive at a defensible business case.

- **Present It**. The various outputs for different ABC roles.

During the course of the presentation, a few additional questions came up from the ABC Financial Services management team.

ABC Manager. The model looks pretty complete. But we don't have a lot of the data you're asking for.

Peter: We've found that few companies have all the data needed. If you don't have data, you can take advantage of our customer experience and industry benchmarks. We recognize that this will give you a coarser level business case estimate; however, a coarse estimate is better than none at all. Moreover, a business case (by definition) deals in uncertainty – projecting value based on current experience, knowledge, and assumptions. So, its real value is as a *decision support tool* as opposed to an absolutely precise prediction of business value; the goal is to guide decision making — influencing project scope, sequence and implementation activities. Moreover, our model provides a flexible vehicle with 'levers' that YOU can pull to evaluate the sensitivity of the business case to varying assumptions. This helps calibrate the risk of your decision in a prudent, business-like way.

Harry Ross (CIO). Our CFO is a hard-nosed finance guy. He's usually only interested in giving us credit for 'hard' cost savings. I'm sure you've run into this issue before. How have you handled it?

Peter. You're right Harry. Many of our customers share the same concern: they are primarily interested in being able to 'do more with less' resources. In the model, we refer to these as 'direct' benefits because they are directly traceable to a budget line item or affect the P&L statement. However, others are also interested in aspects of our solution that will allow them to 'do more with the same' level of resource or mitigate business risks (like regulatory non-compliance penalties or adverse impact of malware infections or phishing attacks on end user productivity). We refer to these benefits as 'indirect.'

Either way our model allows you to distinguish between benefits that lead to 'hard savings' and are applied towards the investment metric calculations and those that are considered 'soft' and excluded from the calculations. Of course, these decisions are strictly up to you, but the model provides you with the flexibility to make them.

Following the presentation, Harry polled the team. It was 'thumbs-up' all around the table. Harry asked Mildred and Peter to make it happen and they scheduled a follow up meeting. Peter explained that this required conducting a working session with the team to select the applicable benefits and to refine the inputs.

CASE STUDY EPISODE 10: Facilitating a Business Case Workshop with Buyer's Team

Collaborating with Mildred and her team to build a defensible business case

The good news for Peter is that building a defensible business case simply requires the same process as described above for creating a value hypothesis. The only difference is that now Peter serves as a facilitator – working with Mildred's team to incorporate their data and assumptions. Peter works with Mildred and her team to revise all of the inputs and revisit the impacts on the investment metrics. This is an iterative process that leads to Mildred being comfortable with the resulting business case. This collaborative approach leads to a defensible business case -- creating the buy-in required to transfer ownership of the resulting business case from Peter to Mildred.

To present the final business case, Peter downloads an executive summary and supporting detail to provide full transparency of all the numbers in the business case. The executive summary is a one-page summary highlighting the key investment metrics (ROI, Payback Period, Net Present Value, and 3-month Cost of Delay) with supporting illustrations showing 3-year cost-benefits and a distribution of business value by various groupings of benefits as described above.

CASE STUDY EPISODE 11: Transferring Ownership of the Business Case to the Economic Buyer

With Mildred and team on board, it was time to deliver the final presentation to Harry and get his feedback. Because Mildred and her team had been intimately involved in building the business case, she agreed to co-present the results with Peter and Susan. Mildred would take the lead and address all the questions related to the selection of benefits and the values used for the various factors involved in quantifying ROI and payback – basically addressing the anticipated question from Harry: 'Where did these numbers come from?'

Peter and Susan were available to clarify the process and address any questions that Harry had with respect to the platform. And Harry did have a few more questions.

> Harry (turning to Mildred): Where did these value statements come from? Are we confident that they are connected to our specific problems and address the concerns in the audit?

> Mildred. Yes, our team made sure that the value statements in the model covered the points made in the audit. We also made sure that we included value statements that connected to our other pain points. So, we're satisfied that this set of value statements represents the greatest potential payback for our investment.

> Harry (turning to Peter). Ok. I'm pleased that the value statements and underlying data and assumptions have been vetted with our team. But some of the assumptions are predicated on benchmark data. What happens if they turn out to be incorrect?

> Peter: The assumptions in the model are easily adjusted. For example, the model is structured so that you can provide a range of improvement values from 'Conservative' to 'Probable' to 'Aggressive.' You may change one or all of these values to explore the sensitivity of the resulting ROI calculation to these changes. The current model reflects what Mildred and team feel are probable improvement values based on the Proof of Value exercise. However, I've prepared the following table to give you a feel for the kind of 'sensitivity analysis' you can do.

Figure 3.9: Using a Sensitivity Analysis to Calibrate Investment Risk

Improvement Factor	Discount Rate = 12%	
	Projected ROI (Percent)	Projected Payback (months)
Conservative	160%	12.6
Probable	234%	10.8
Aggressive	270%	8.2

The table shows the impact on ROI and payback period for the various improvement factor levels. Given this early version of the model, one can conclude that the ROI is in the 200% range with a payback period of about one year. Of course, there are also other 'levers' in the model that you can pull (e.g., discount rate, benefit phasing, anticipated driver factor growth / decline rates) to analyze sensitivity – further helping you assess the risk of the decision to invest.

Harry. OK. I'd like a few days to look at the model in more detail. Mildred, it's important that we can quantify the risk we've got in realizing the ROI you've come up with.

Peter (interjecting). Absolutely. And as we discussed early on, keep in mind that there are a variety of 'levers' in the model that you can work with to ratchet down the resulting metrics to account for risk factors such as schedule slippage and user acceptance. You can make these adjustments at the benefit level (e.g., by adjusting improvement factors) or at the model level (e.g., by adjusting discount rate, annual benefit realization percent, etc.)

By the end of the week, Harry and Mildred completed their due diligence. They did ratchet down the model to a point where Harry felt completely confident that he could justify the investment to the CFO. Given the urgency of the CEO's concern about their vulnerabilities, Harry got an audience quickly. He got the go-head to proceed with the CyberSecure investment.

The result: Mildred got the tools she needed to do the job, her end users were delighted, and Peter closed a multi-million-dollar order for CyberSecure software. A win-win situation for all involved. Afterwards, Mildred remarked to Peter: "This is the best business case I have ever seen presented at our company."

CASE STUDY EPISODE 12: Measuring Post-implementation Value Realized

At the outset of their business relationship, Peter Sellers and Mildred Pierce agreed to establish a formal 'Customer Success Program' to ensure that ABC Financial expectations were being met as the rollout of the CyberSecure solution proceeded. Given Susan Smart's involvement as the CyberSecure Value Practitioner throughout the business case development process, all agreed that she would serve as the CyberSecure Customer Success Manager for this effort.

To begin, Susan organized a call with Mildred and Harry Ross (CIO) to present the program and cover the following agenda topics.

- Review SOW Deliverable Agreement. Ensure that all parties understand the terms and conditions of the agreement.

- Review Progress to Date / Current Status. Ensure that the current business case accurately represents the expected outcomes.

- Define Success. Agree on the specific metrics that will be used to monitor progress and measure success.

- Identify Risks & Challenges

- Determine Rollout Approach / Enablement Best Practices. Agree on the staging and sequence of tasks required to deploy the CyberSecure solution to the end user community.

- Agree on Timeline & Upcoming Activities

- Designate Key Contacts & Establish Cadence

As a result of this call, all agreed on establishing a cadence for two specific events:

1. **Formal Value Realization Assessments** would be conducted on a quarterly basis. The focus of these assessments would be on gathering insight into planned versus actual business value achievement to date while also collecting feedback from the customer regarding their experience and sentiment. Following the assessment, the results will be evaluated to recommend appropriate corrective actions or opportunities for value expansion.

2. **Quarterly Value Reviews (QVR).** A counterpart to the Quarterly Business Review, the QVR provides a forum to present the results of the assessments, discuss recommendations, and agree on appropriate actions. This review session also provides a way to gather insights, testimonials, and evidence of success to be used in future value analyses.

Three months following implementation, Susan engages Mildred to conduct a Value Realization assessment. The assessment showed that the value realized to date was closely tracking the projection. However, Mildred and Susan agreed that the solution rollout took a little longer than expected. They're comfortable that with end user training now complete, the business model and plan is still valid.

Other Important Customer Engagement Tips

The Hard versus Soft Benefit Conversation

A frequent topic of conversation in building a business case is how benefits are treated and weighted in terms of relative importance to justify investing in B2B solutions. Often this leads to a debate of 'hard' versus 'soft' benefits. The opening gambit for some buyers is 'we only consider hard benefits' when justifying an investment. Which of course begs the question: 'how do you define 'hard'? It's actually a great question that strikes at the heart of credible value messaging, and the reason why c-level buyers don't take claims of 600% ROI with 3-month payback seriously. So, let's begin with some definitions.

- **Hard Benefits**, sometimes referred to as 'Direct' or 'Tangible' benefits, are the line items that directly impact P&L. They are typically found as line items in budgets or project plans. Hence, they are *'measurable'* and someone can be held *accountable* for performance. Examples include FTE (Full Time Equivalent) labor costs, annual contract service expenses, hardware or software expenses. The mantra for this type of benefit is 'Doing more with less.'

- **Soft Benefits**, often referred to as 'Indirect' or 'Qualitative' benefits, are line items that do not show up in budgets. Typically, they are risks that would be mitigated to a degree by making an investment in a B2B solution. For example, mitigating the risk of end user productivity or revenue loss, customer disloyalty, or regulatory non-compliance penalties. The tagline for this type of benefit is 'Doing more with the same.' The point being that existing people can be reallocated to more strategic work, perhaps increasing revenue or improving the customer experience. These are harder to measure.

Now let's consider some fundamental principles and associated practices that might guide you through this sometimes-sticky conversation.

Principle 1. Become Your Customer's Trusted Advisor

Never assume you know what the customer means by 'hard' versus 'soft.' Establishing a Trusted Advisor relationship with your customer requires clarification on what Benefits are 'hard' versus 'soft.' That way a meaningful measurement baseline can be established. Here are some lessons learned to consider.

- **Focus on the buyer's desire to change.** Don't get caught up in philosophical debates about hard versus soft costs. Rather, understand the nature of the change the buyer is committed to making and then focus on the best way to quantify the potential benefits realized from those changes.

- **Reframe the conversation**. Challenge the status quo and push for alternative ways to move the needle. Productivity measurement can be applied to any form of capital or human resource and knowing how productivity efficiencies align with competitive advantage and bottom-line results should be where the conversation starts.

- **Gain insight into the buyer business transformation strategy and drivers.** Understanding the customer's strategy and expected outcomes will dictate how you position benefits. In some cases, you may need to shift the conversation from cost savings to revenue growth. A high revenue growth company views benefits differently than a mature, slow growth business with a need for cost savings. Are mergers and acquisitions part of the strategy? If so, a productivity argument can be made such as, 'you can assimilate the acquisition without the need to hire more people, resulting in a tangible and measurable cost avoidance.'

- **Go with the flow.** Ultimately, the buyer decides what's 'hard' versus 'soft', not you. Wait for the buyer to request a breakdown, don't volunteer it. Once the decision is made, always lead with hard benefits. While soft benefits can be quantified, they should come along for the ride. Soft benefits may be treated as 'Other (Qualitative) Considerations' in your business case. Keep in mind that soft benefits may play a larger role with quality or process-oriented customers.

Principle 2. Reposition the nature of the Benefit. Sometimes it makes sense to think of a benefit in a different way. For example, instead of defining the benefit in terms of 'FTE (Full Time Equivalent) Labor Savings', define and position it as 'Cost per Event'. Thus, if a call center call currently costs $5 per call, and you can claim a 20% productivity improvement, then the Cost per Call is reduced to $4. On one million calls per year, that's a $1M savings.

Principle 3. Deal with Push Back Confidently. Expect buyers to push back on the productivity 'doing more with the same' scenario. This conversation usually turns on three possibilities.

- **Natural attrition or terminations** — For buyers looking to reduce costs, turn productivity improvement into actual FTE (headcount) reduction. FTE reduction can be handled by terminations and natural attrition.

- **Reduce future hiring needs** — For high growth companies, this can be treated as FTE cost avoidance.

- **Opportunity cost** — More projects making their way through the queue, reallocating resources to growth initiatives rather than keeping the lights on.

Principle 4. Service delivery people need to bridge the 'expectations gap' between the buyer and seller. If not careful, a service delivery person can get caught up in the expectations debate between buyer and seller. As a service delivery person, be sure to set measurable baseline expectations at proposal time, gain agreement on the baseline collection of metrics that will be used to measure success, and periodically measure value realized.

Principle 5. Ask the right questions

- Two questions may help frame the hard vs soft discussion with a buyer. First, what could they do with the time saved? And second, what is the next best alternative? Sometimes FTE savings are hard to discuss, but when framed in the lens of 'what would it cost to outsource the work to a service provider,' it makes quantifying the benefit more compelling.

- What business drivers are you measured on? For example: number of new customers, call center calls, security breaches, IT staff size, etc. Challenge your buyer; ask 'what if you could generate more revenue with the same resource?'

- What additional goals cannot get accomplished without increased productivity, such as handling backlog, reducing project idle times, or preparing key deliverables?

- What are your company-stated business goals with respect to productivity gains? How do you treat direct (hard) versus indirect (soft) benefits in your business case? Are you only interested in saving real dollars by FTE reduction either from attrition or layoffs? Or are you willing to ascribe a financial value by repurposing labor to more strategic pursuits through process optimization?

Bottom line: Value comes in many forms, and benefit discussions can take many directions. It is essential to build the right relationship with the customer to understand their needs and have the conversations that allow all parties to understand where benefits become business value and how that value can be measured.

Proof of Value versus Proof of Concept

Often Demos and Proofs of Concept are designed to show WHAT the product will do and HOW it works. They fail to clarify WHY these capabilities matter. Anything that is 'Extra' that a seller thinks is "Good" may or may not be useful in the eyes of the Buyer. If you are not focused on WHY your capabilities are critical to buyer success, then the WHAT and HOW your product works is simply not relevant to the conversation.

Thus, there is a difference between a Proof of Concept and Proof of Value. While a POC is designed to demonstrate that your solution performs as advertised in the customer's environment, a Proof of Value does this and more. A POV should be specifically designed to bridge the gap between the capabilities of your solution and its business value. You can do this by helping the buyer align and synchronize their technical and business due diligence processes. It is important that at the onset of the POV both the buyer and seller agree upon a specific timeline and a tangible set of success criteria that are achievable in that timeframe. Here's how.

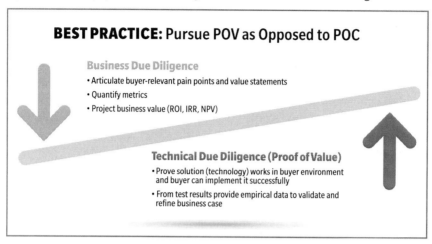

You already know it is essential to gain the buyer's team consensus on the Value Statements that drive the investment decision. Will the investment contribute to revenue growth, cost reduction, productivity gains, or risk mitigation? If so, in what way and how will these business outcomes be measured?

With this value framework in hand, you can align the technical objectives of the Proof of Value with the customer pain points and corresponding business value statements to ensure that you are testing only these key business value 'hypotheses' and gathering appropriate empirical data to help populate your business case model — overriding as many of the default values in the model as possible.

By constraining the POV to demonstrate and test only those capabilities required to support the agreed-to value statements your sales engineering team limits the time and effort required to conduct the test, compress the time it takes to complete the decision making process, and ensure that the underlying data and assumptions in the model are as realistic as possible.

From this point forward, you have enough data to present the results of the POV along with a compelling business case. However, there are a few other things to keep in mind when planning a Proof of Value.

- Know your audience. Often you are demoing to more than one buyer role. Just as you should create persona-relevant business case assets, you should prepare for the various roles of individuals involved in the POV.

- Hone in on the specific use-cases and accompanying client stories that are most relevant to the various buyer roles. Make it easy on your prospects to follow. Avoid making the buyer have to do all the mental gymnastics of "imagine if."

- Make it clear what capabilities are being demonstrated to address each specific pain point – value statement pair in your business case. You only need to demo capabilities connected to the value statements that resonate with the buyer.

- Demonstrations should be structured so that you have deep dive and lite versions.

This completes our discussion of how to transform your organization to a differentiated value selling model. Now we are ready to move on to describe how to 'refreeze' this new way of doing business by managing customer success.

PART 4
MANAGING CUSTOMER SUCCESS

Part 4. Managing Customer Success

Perfection is not attainable. But if we chase perfection, we can catch excellence. – Vince Lombardi

Goals of Customer Success Management: 'Refreezing' Transformation

You've now successfully launched the CVM Program – '<u>unfreezing</u>' the existing culture along the way. You've validated the program with customers and buyers by collaborating with sales teams to test and refine the value models and sales assets – completing the <u>transformation</u> from a product to a differentiated value selling model. Now it's time to ensure that the transformation sticks; it's time to lock in ('<u>refreeze</u>') the new CVM approach.

To make this happen, we turn again to the key organizational change management goals.

- How do we sustain the *motivation* to help promote success and continuously improve the program?

- What practices work? Which practices are not effective and need to be fixed?

- What additional *enablement* is required? How do we onboard hew people?

- How do we continuously *reinforce* this behavior to make the change stick?

Let's explore how this is done, beginning with success measures and challenges and then introducing best practices.

CVM Program Success Measures

An effective Customer Value Management Program is a win-win proposition for both the <u>seller</u> (your internal stakeholders from sales, marketing, product management, customer success, and others) and the <u>buyer</u> of your B2B solutions (the accounts for whom you build business cases and conduct value realization assessments).

Buyers need help in justifying investments and measuring value realized. Both parties recognize that their keys to success are (a) an effective business case to justify investments and (b) the ability to measure and showcase business value post solution implementation. Sellers need to be prepared to give it to them in a way that satisfies their business goals of profitable new deals, license / subscription renewals, and increased cross-sell / upsell opportunities.

The opportunity for you, as a Trusted Advisor to both parties, is to ensure <u>their</u> mutual success. <u>Your</u> success in achieving this goal will likely be measured by answering the questions in the following table.

Figure 4.1: CVM Program Success Measures

Customer Satisfaction	Stakeholder Satisfaction

Are Buyer's investments in your solutions achieving the expected value and ROI?
 	
• What evidence do you have of value realized (the perception as well as the reality)?
• Are customers willing to collaborate on ROI Case Studies and provide testimonials?
• Have you considered using Net Promoter Score (NPS) to gauge customer satisfaction?
	Is the CVM program satisfying your internal stakeholder advocacy network?
	• Are sales teams adopting and using the CVM models and assets as expected to close more and bigger deals, faster? Have you achieved the ROI projected in the original business case – quantifying (for example):
	   ◦ Improved Conversion Rate opportunities to forecast
	   ◦ Reduced Sales Cycle Time and Effort
	   ◦ Improved Percentage Close Rate
	   ◦ Improved Average Sales Price (reduced Discount Rate)
	• Has Marketing leveraged CVM-generated assets to do targeted account-based marketing leading to:
	   ◦ Higher Marketing Campaign Response Rates
	   ◦ Increased Marketing Qualified Leads (MQLs) generated
	   ◦ Higher Conversion of MQLs to real opportunities
	• Has Customer Success achieved their goals of renewals and account expansion?
	   ◦ Improved Retention Rate
	   ◦ Reduced Churn
	   ◦ Increased Cross-sell/up-sell

These are the measures of CVM Program success. Addressing these questions requires formalizing and sustaining your relationships with all parties, making sure that you are properly managing expectations and showcasing value. To achieve these goals, you need to be prepared to address the following challenges.

Challenges

'Refreezing' a newly activated business value-driven culture is the final step (see *Launching an Agile Customer Value Management Program* above, the *Manage it* step). Let's revisit these challenges and assess your current state of readiness.

<u>Setting and Managing expectations</u>. Recall that setting expectations requires a number of actions:

1. Identify the key stakeholders: This group of individuals represent your network of advocacy. Understand their specific roles and needs with respect to CVM.

2. Gain executive sponsorship: At an operational level your sponsor will likely be the CRO. In addition to this individual, you should also line up a Champion (perhaps VP, Sales Engineering or Sales Operations) who will help coordinate activities with the stakeholder community. Ideally, getting the CEO and CFO involved early on is beneficial. At a minimum they should be aware of the CVM initiative. Getting their substantive input to the program will move the program along more quickly.

3. Build a formal business case and program charter: clarify program expectations, governance, critical success factors and key activities. An accompanying schedule and assignments helps (a) lock in the commitment to get the resources and funding you need; (b) provides the baseline metrics for measuring program success; and (c) properly sets manageable expectations.

Overcoming resistance to change. Like any other major transformational initiative, you should expect and anticipate resistance from field sales teams to using the CVM platform. Some of this resistance is natural – people are nervous about changing to something they're not totally familiar or comfortable with. Don't be discouraged by this; assess the resistance for valid and potentially constructive changes. For example, the initial value model may miss important benefits or not address specific sales situations. This may lead to a lack of confidence and adoption, exacerbating resistance and leading some stakeholders to overreact and want to "throw the baby out with the bath water." Handled properly, constructive feedback can be leveraged to improve the accuracy and effectiveness of the program. Moreover, your willingness to make improvements underscores a 'let's-build-this-program-together' mindset. Here are a few ideas to help you turn initial resistance into a positive step forward for the program:

1. Conduct pilots with 'friendly' customers before releasing the program to the field. During enablement training, include feedback from customers and include a case study that walks through how the CVM process was used to quantify and showcase value realized.

2. Properly set expectations with CVM end users. During enablement, when introducing end users to the program, be open about the current state of the value model and ask for feedback from the field on its use. Remind the field of Vince Lombardi's advice: *"Perfection is not attainable. But if we chase perfection, we can catch excellence."*

3. Create a 'let's-do-this-together' mindset. As part of enablement training, use a case study and workshop to engage field sales teams in helping build out the content for the program.

Measuring Value Realized. Just as customers need to measure value realized from the implementation of your solutions, you need to measure and report the value realized from the CVM Program. To this end (recalling the *CVM Launch* stage), you already established a credible methodology and ROI model to use as the measurement baseline.

Keep in mind that measuring CVM value realized is a very important piece of the 'reinforce' part of the equation. Customers and stakeholders need to understand what business value has been achieved. Showcasing value will encourage higher adoption. Thus, it is important to establish a cadence for measuring and reporting value – perhaps through formal Quarterly Value Reviews (QVRs).

Figure 4.2: Managing the Demand-Success-Improvement Cycle

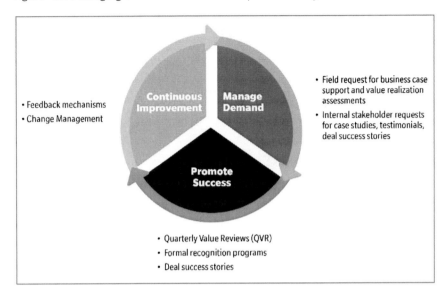

Managing the Demand-Success-Improvement Cycle. Success breeds success. As the CVM Program gains traction, you need to be prepared to manage an increase in demand. Demand comes from multiple sources: (1) the field will request support for deals in the pipeline as well as showcasing value for existing customers and (2) internal stakeholders will recognize the need for additional collateral that results from buyer and customer interactions. For example, marketing is interested in ROI success stories, case studies, and empirical data that reflects business value that customers have experienced. Sales teams are interested in lessons learned from customer interactions; for example: which benefits resonate with buyers; deal success stories that clarify value-selling best practices. Thus, there is a need to establish processes that routinely captures this information and provides a basis for engaging stakeholders, sorting out priorities for support, and managing expectations.

The flip side of managing demand, is generating demand. There is no better way to do this than to consistently promote success by showing what GREAT looks like. Case studies, internal deal success stories, formal Quarterly Value Reviews, and formal recognition programs are ways to make this happen.

Lastly, while perfection is not attainable, continuous improvement most certainly is. Mechanisms needs to be established to routinely collect feedback from customers and internal stakeholder on every aspect of the CVM Program including value models, sales assets, and customer engagement process. Given this feedback, change management becomes an essential process to ensure that changes are made in a systematic, non-intrusive way.

Let's drill down to explore the specific practices required to address these challenges.

Guiding Principles and Best Practices

"Change before you have to"
– Jack Welch, former CEO, General Electric Company

To address these challenges and achieve success, it's important to think in terms of 'organizational change' as well as 'process and technology change'. The figure below suggests a framework that embraces a holistic change management approach to help manage the CVM Program in the steady state.

1. **MEASURE IT**. As Peter Drucker once commented: *"What gets measured gets improved."* Thus, measuring stakeholder usage and adoption, gathering feedback, and assessing effectiveness of results (win and renewal rates, reduced churn, customer satisfaction) is the starting point.

2. **PRESENT IT** requires establishing a routine cadence of review meetings with managers to showcase results and recommend course corrections as appropriate.

3. **PROMOTE IT** involves keeping the program front-and-center in everyone's mind.

4. **IMPROVE IT** requires institutionalizing all the processes required to manage demand and changes to content and infrastructure.

Figure 4.3: Framework for Ensuring Customer Success

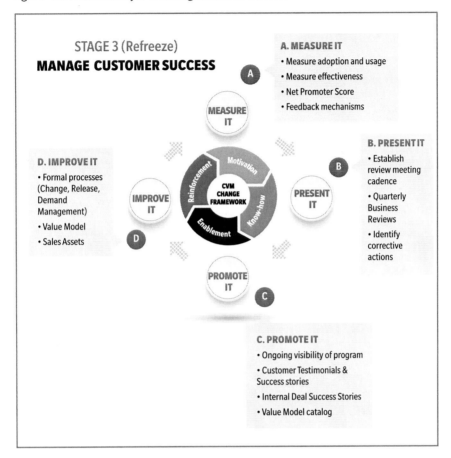

Measure and Present It

The Measure and Present steps are critical to achieving the goals of sustaining momentum and keeping everyone fired up to embrace and improve the program. There are two key success factors involved in making this happen: (1) continuous involvement of executive leadership and first line managers and (2) ongoing feedback from internal stakeholders and customers. To this end, consider establishing the following practices.

Ensure Continuous Management Involvement at All Levels

It's critical to gain up-front agreement with executive management on baseline metrics for measuring program success. Even after your first successes, it's important to keep the CVM program front and center in everyone's mind. To this end:

1. **Promote adoption** by providing ongoing visibility of the CVM Program — including adoption levels, model usage, success stories, and issues requiring resolution.

2. **Conduct periodic reviews** with sales, marketing, product management, and customer success. This requires:
   - Setting thresholds at each forecast stage where you expect 100% compliance (e.g., parameters around size of deal)
   - Routinely tracking and reporting adoption progress, then taking appropriate corrective action. The figure below provides an example of a Usage and Adoption Report. This type of analysis can be a helpful way to prompt discussion of the month-to-month variance and learning what works and doing more of that.

   - Reporting business case status for each deal. For example: account name; projected ROI; stage of sales process (system projected; account team refined; customer engaged; deal won / lost).

   - Conducting monthly reviews with customer sales management. Encourage friendly competition through routine reporting of usage and adoption by sales team and each team member.

   - Conducting quarterly reviews with marketing / product management to get their feedback on the program, suggestions for new assets (e.g., case studies, testimonials), and insight into forthcoming new products or enhancements that may affect models.

   - Periodic results / lessons learned from Value Realization Assessments.

Figure 4.4: Reporting CVM Usage and Adoption

3. **Certify First Line Sales Managers as coaches**. Managers should challenge reps at deal inspection time – including a discussion of the business case status for each deal. Who is Champion? What are key 'pain point – value statement pairs' driving deal? To help managers, automatic notifications should be issued whenever a change occurs in the progress of a business case for each deal.

Get Direct Feedback from End Users

Perhaps the most important input to measurement and management reporting is the direct feedback you will get from field sales teams, customers, and partners.

1. One of your great challenges is overcoming resistance to change. You are bound to get resistance from the field to using something new and imperfect because of missing Benefits or situations and inadequate benchmark data, to name a few. Thus, it's important to understand the cause of the resistance.

   • Are the models missing benefits?

   • Are the benefits unclear? Perhaps they need more descriptive names or enriched explanatory content.

   • Are the commonly encountered selling situations accounted for sufficiently? For example, are variations due to industry, geography, or use cases properly reflected in the value model?

   • Do the benefits have sufficient proof points (evidence that the default values for the various factors are realistic)?

   • Is the usage of benchmark data appropriate? Are the sources of the benchmark data provided for reference?

- Is the feedback coming from a particular region? Solution area? Sales team? Users? Does the source of the resistance give any hint as to the reason for the resistance?

Reemphasize key caveats about the use of the solution value model(s). For example, consider making the following points:

- We know that the model is not perfect – and it never will be. Quantifying solution value is not an exact science. The important thing is to open the door to a provocative conversation with a buyer and provide a directional sense of business value. A value program is best viewed as a decision support program where the value platform is intended to provide the content required for "telling your value story" more so than it is intended to provide totally accurate numbers.

- As we get more direct customer experience, the model will be refined further. We can expect to add or delete benefits along the way. We can expect to refine values for various factors and assumptions as we engage customers in different industries. And we will collect more proof points and case studies from customer experience that will enhance the rigor of the model going forward. Remember: your goal is an agile value management approach. Agility means getting a usable capability off the ground quickly and refining it over time as you get direct customer and stakeholder feedback.

2. Identify a Subject Matter Expert (SME) as the owner of each value model. Consider having a product manager own each value model. This will boost the comfort and confidence of the field that the model is valid and that someone is accountable for keeping the model up to date as enhancements to the solution are made over time.

3. Establish processes to routinely get actionable feedback from the field to help improve the efficacy of all solution value models.

   - Use Sales quarterly business reviews and deal inspections as sources of feedback on effectiveness of solution value models. Ask what changes are needed with models.

Management can collect suggestions and / or coach as appropriate.

- Conduct 'reality checks' on the use of the models. For example, through bi-weekly usage tracking (number of touches; number of value propositions created / month); assess who's using the model(s); who's not; who is getting better. What assumptions and benchmarks are typically used?

4. Offer easy-to-use tools to collect feedback

- Use Chatter, Slack, or another collaboration platform for gathering input on needed value model refreshes or improvements.

- Establish a 'make-my-life-easier' suggestions box – perhaps using a benefit rating scale to capture end user opinion on the importance and relevance of each benefit to buyers.

5. Explore customer willingness to provide testimonials and collaborate on ROI case studies.

6. Use Net Promoter Score (NPS) approach to measure stakeholder and customer satisfaction.

7. Extend the reach of CVM to partners. Engage partners as another important stakeholder. Understand how they quantify value (as they likely have their own business case methods and tools), exchange perspectives, and offer to collaborate and share CVM IP.

Promote It

This requires packaging knowledge and lessons learned to enhance current team skills and onboard new people. It requires communicating what works and what doesn't as well as celebrating successes.

Once formal enablement training is complete, the 'call to action' should require that each sales rep identify at least one account to engage with the CVM Program. These accounts provide the opportunity for 1:1 coaching. Early successes from these engagements provide the basis for case study success stories and recognizing the sales rep's accomplishment (perhaps as part of the Quarterly Value Review agenda). In fact, it's a good idea to formalize the recognition program and the way you collect and publish success stories.

To this end, you should establish a process and template to facilitate collection of data that clarifies how CVM is being used to help close deals in the field. For example, you might publish *internal* Deal Success Stories on a quarterly basis. These stories are 1-2-page write-ups that highlight individual rep success in closing a deal. This includes a testimonial from the rep on the efficacy of the CVM Program as well as lessons learned. The goal: encourage full team participation (100% compliance) by leveraging lessons learned and best practices in using the CVM process and assets.

Recognize that enablement is never-ending. It's also an opportunity to promote and expand the use of CVM beyond the sales organization into the marketing and customer success organizations.

And always keep in mind that people are at different stages on the learning curve; so, training and enablement needs to be adjusted accordingly for different roles. As mentioned earlier, first line sales managers need to evolve into effective coaches and everyone needs to get sharper using the full tool set.

Improve It

Here you institutionalize all the processes required to manage demand and changes to content and infrastructure. Generally speaking, it makes sense to centralize content management. This means establishing formal processes and teams of individuals responsible for engineering and maintaining all solution value models – making it clear who owns a given value model along with the go-to person for questions about model.

Among the practices that need to be considered are:

1. **Demand Management**. How do you manage demand for business case support and sales assets? Keep in mind that demand comes from a number our sources, including:

   - Field support for business cases

   - Marketing will be interested in collecting first-hand customer experience information for case study material and sales collateral

   - Product Management will value feedback from customers to help define requirements for product roadmaps.

2. **Content Change Management**. Establish standardized methods, processes and procedures to facilitate efficient and prompt handling of all changes, and maintain the proper balance between the need for change and the potential detrimental impact of changes. Changes to value models come from a number of sources.

   - Customers and buyers provide feedback on the relative importance and relevance of benefits in the models. Value Realization assessments provide empirical data that affects the baseline value in the various factors.

   - Problems with the models, assets, or supporting CVM infrastructure that need to be fixed

   - New products created internally or as the result of acquisitions

   - Upgrades to the CVM Automation platform.

For organizations that support multiple value models, it helps to create a Model Reference Catalog. This should be a standard output of a CVM platform that clarifies each benefit in the model, including description, factors used, and assumption details.

3. **Release Management**. A sister discipline to Change Management, the goals of release management include:

   - Planning the rollout of CVM software and value model updates

   - Effectively communicating and managing customer expectations during the planning and rollout of new releases

   - Controlling the distribution and installation of changes

   - Formal model release / refresh process and schedule (perhaps annually)

4. **Formalize Processes for CVM Automation Platform Administration**. Recognize that, in addition to content management, the capabilities of the CVM automation platform you select will also improve over time. Let your voice be heard. Participate in advisory sessions and get your input into the roadmap for improvements.

5. **Security Management**. Because Value Models are designed to differentiate your value from competitors, they represent a form of intellectual property that must be protected. This is another important consideration in the selection of your CVM automation platform. It's also the reason a central repository of value models representing a 'single source of truth' lends itself to a more secure environment than spreadsheets owned by individuals who take their knowledge with them should they leave the company.

PART 5
SUMMARY:
ARE YOU READY?

Part 5. Summary: Are You Ready?

"One of the most important lessons about crossing the chasm is that the task ultimately requires achieving an unusual degree of company unity during the crossing period." – Geoffrey A. Moore, Crossing the Chasm

First published in 1991, Geoffrey Moore's ground-breaking treatise *Crossing the Chasm* has had a significant and lasting impact on the way organization's assimilate disruptive technology innovation. While his book focuses on how to market and sell products to customers in various stages of the technology adoption lifecycle (innovators, early adopters, early majority, late majority, and laggards), it also has implications for launching and leveraging any major technology innovation within an organization. Which brings us to the connection to launching and sustaining an agile Customer Value Management Program.

At its core, a Customer Value Management Program is about the 'analog to digital transformation' of value management. The 'old way' (homegrown Excel spreadsheets, requiring experts to use, and significant manual effort) will no longer cut it in today's fast-paced, highly competitive world. Sellers and buyers are evolving to a 'new way' to engage — requiring a secure, scalable, self-service, value automation platform with multiple applications to support the complete value journey — from value discovery to business case creation to measuring and showcasing value realized.

Clearly, this next generation Customer Value Management (CVM) platform is a disruptive technology – akin to the impact that enterprise-scale applications like Customer Relationship Management (CRM) or Enterprise Resource Planning (ERP) have had on businesses since their introduction. In fact, Customer Value Management is increasingly viewed as the logical extension to traditional CRM systems.

Herein lies the opportunity for the Value Practitioner – scaling the delivery of customer value across the enterprise to help create

GREAT buyer-seller experiences. As Geoffrey Moore points out, crossing the chasm requires "achieving an unusual degree of company unity across the crossing period." Taking advantage of this opportunity is what we mean by 'unleashing customer value' — an opportunity for you to be a hero to the entire enterprise, not just for a single opportunity.

Making this happen requires methodically walking through a series of stages – unfreezing an existing mindset, transforming the organization to a 'better future', and refreezing the new culture. In each stage, we described the goals and practices required to achieve 'unity' across both internal and external stakeholders.

To summarize, these practices include:

- Creating internal 'company unity' by selling the vision and plan for a formal, properly branded CVM Program. This includes creating a network of advocacy among senior executives and stakeholders in the sales, marketing, product management, and customer success organizations.

- Launching a formal CVM Program by creating the right content, for the right people, at the right altitude and scaling delivery using a secure, next generation value automation platform.

- Engaging buyers and customers through the entire customer 'value journey' — from value discovery to business case development through showcasing value realized.

- Ensuring continuous improvement by capturing feedback, celebrating success, and fine-tuning content and processes.

We close this book with a tool to help you assess your readiness – keeping in mind the words of Peter Drucker: *"The best way to predict the future is to create it; if you want something new, you have to stop doing something old."*

Each of the line items below represents a prescribed best practice that we have explained herein. As suggested, simply check the box to the right that indicates where you stand relative to the practice.

Figure 5.1: CVM Readiness Self-Assessment Survey

BEST PRACTICES ASSESSMENT CRITERIA	AGILITY				
	Not Started	One-third Complete	Half-way Complete	Two-thirds Complete	Complete (world class)
	1	2	3	4	5
SELLING CVM INTERNALLY (refer to Part 2 for detailed discussion)					
I have full support of an <u>Executive Sponsor and Champion</u> for a branded CVM Program					
I have stakeholder agreement that the scope of CVM should support the full end-to-end customer engagement process engagement (value discovery → value delivery → value realization)					
I have aligned and integrated CVM with the preferred sales process and frameworks (e.g., MEDDICC, Challenger, etc.)					
I have an approved <u>budget and plan</u>					
I have an internal <u>network of advocacy</u> including sales, marketing, and customer success teams					
I have stakeholder agreement on <u>success measures</u>					
I have an agreed upon program charter that specifies expected outcomes, critical success factors, program governance, key activities and schedules					

BEST PRACTICES ASSESSMENT CRITERIA	AGILITY				
	Not Started	One-third Complete	Half-way Complete	Two-thirds Complete	Complete (world class)
	1	2	3	4	5
LAUNCHING CVM PROGRAM INTERNALLY (refer to Part 2 for detailed discussion)					
I have captured the collective knowledge of internal stakeholders and gained agreement on the baseline solution value model(s) that underpin the program					
I have identified an owner for each value model					
I have established a secure, self-service, scalable value automation platform that supports the full customer value life cycle					
I have created buyer persona-specific sales asset templates that will be used to engage buyers and customers					
I have agreement on the CVM customer engagement process and its alignment with the sales process					
I have validated the program process and value model(s) with at least 3 'friendly' customers					
I have developed all the collateral reps need to 'sell' the program to buyers and customers (e.g., elevator pitch, CVM Program fact sheet, intro PPT, FAQs, etc.)					
I have built and delivered a role-based enablement program					

BEST PRACTICES ASSESSMENT CRITERIA	AGILITY				
	Not Started	One-third Complete	Half-way Complete	Two-thirds Complete	Complete (world class)
	1	2	3	4	5
I have empowered first line sales managers as effective value coaches					
I have established the processes to capture stakeholder feedback and manage demand and change for all elements of the program (value model, sales assets, process)					
ENGAGING BUYERS TO COLLABORATE ON BUSINESS CASE (refer to Part 3 for detailed discussion)					
I have developed a repeatable end-to-end process for engaging customers with a value hypothesis, formal business case, and value realization assessment					
I have established a 'deal desk' to coach sales teams on leveraging CVM assets					
I have synchronized the Proof of Value (technical due diligence) and Business Case development (business due diligence) processes					
SHOWCASING VALUE REALIZED WITH CUSTOMERS (refer to Part 3 for detailed discussion)					
I have a credible process and methodology for measuring and showcasing value realized					
I have established a checkpoint review					

BEST PRACTICES ASSESSMENT CRITERIA	AGILITY				
	Not Started	One-third Complete	Half-way Complete	Two-thirds Complete	Complete (world class)
	1	2	3	4	5
cadence with the Economic Buyer and Champion					
I ensure continuous involvement of Sales leadership by routinely promoting successes					
MANAGING CVM STAKEHOLDER SUCCESS (refer to Part 4 for detailed discussion)					
I have established a continuous improvement process for all elements of CVM (value models, sales assets, enablement training, customer engagement process)					
I have established a routine review CVM Program Checkpoint review cadence internally, with the CVM executive sponsor and champion					
I have formalized the CVM feedback process with internal stakeholders					
I have established a Recognition program to promote success stories					

As illustrated below, using this type of self-assessment checkpoint, provides you with an interesting perspective on how you stack up against best practices.

Figure 5.2: Displaying Your Organization's Customer Value Management Readiness

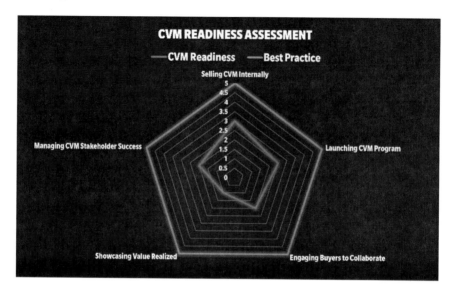

Recall at the outset of this book we explained how building an agile Customer Value Management Program presented an excellent career opportunity for value professionals. In addition to helping calibrate your organization's readiness, the area between the lines also helps visualize the challenge and associated career opportunity for you to contribute to the success of the business.

Keep in mind the words of entrepreneur Chris Grosser: *'Opportunities don't happen. You create them.'* In this book we have distilled decades of experience into a practical collection of frameworks and proven practices that will help you take customer value management to another level. We also explained why establishing a secure, self-service, software-enabled platform that supports the complete customer value cycle is a critical success factor. We hope that these insights will help you take advantage of this opportunity and make something GREAT happen for your organization and you personally.

PART 6
EPILOGUE

EPILOGUE

The Future of Value Management
– The Next 10 Years
Jim Berryhill, CEO & Co-Founder, DecisionLink
With Insight from Chris Dowse, Global Sr Director,
Value Management, ServiceNow

My friend Joe Sexton was President of AppDynamics; he is the hero of their meteoric rise from just over $10 million in annual revenue to a $3.8 billion exit to Cisco. Those who know him call his sayings "Joe-isms". He has a lot of them. They are straight-forward, salt of the earth truths. One of my favorite Joe-isms is, "the two most important words in Customer Relationship Management (CRM) are 'customer' and 'relationship', and customer relationships are exclusively based on CUSTOMER VALUE." Truer words have rarely been spoken.

While this book is about the here and now of Customer Value, I'm most excited about its future. Five years ago, there were hardly 5,000 value professionals on LinkedIn. Today, there are over 50,000. The growth of the value professionals continues on an amazing trajectory.

The real story for Customer Value Management (CVM) is much like the growth of CRM.

In 1990, most sales activity and relationship tracking were done with pen and paper. Some sales professionals used a PC with an early spreadsheet or a rudimentary application like ACT! to keep name, address, phone and basic text data organized. CRM was a nascent marketplace, under $10 million.

By 2000, the CRM market had grown to $1 billion and by 2010 it was up to $15 billion. Today, CRM is the largest software market, valued at $40 billion. And by 2025, it's projected to be $80 billion. Similar to the growth of the automobile, in a short period of time, everybody had a car. In a short period of time, every business used a CRM.

Customer Value will be like this. Soon, ***every organization will have a value management program, and everybody will be proficient in communicating value***. I like to call it "the democratization of value." Value won't just be leveraged by salespeople; it will be commonplace in every customer-facing role across every organization – from marketing, to sales, to partner channels and customer success.

Chris Dowse is one of the leading thinkers and practitioners of value in the industry. Chris serves as the Global Sr Director of the Value Management Program at ServiceNow; he brings great insight to the future of Value Management:

"Pondering the future of Value Management, I am reminded of a quote by the famous sci-fi author William Gibson – *"The future is already here – it's just not evenly distributed".*

Distribution. Uneven Distribution! The key challenge for the value management discipline is how to understand and share benefits across a very complex stakeholder landscape. More specifically, there are three critical distributions that need to be rebalanced:

Power. As technology buyers and sellers build a successful partnership over time, power shifts in terms of whose benefits will drive forward joint success. To be impactful, value management practitioners will need to understand and manage both organizational and individual benefits across the entire adoption lifecycle. Today, most companies struggle with the first and overlook the second entirely.

Insight. While data science practices are finding their way into many aspects of business management, they are quite lacking in the value management arena. There is a significant opportunity for Machine Learning-created insights to power smart-selling and accelerate value realization by revealing "personalized" adoption-value critical paths for each customer.

Confidence. Long gone are the days when value conversations can be delivered by a small group of professional "value engineers" only – business is too fast, and experts are too costly. As companies attempt to scale the ability to deliver value conversations across the entire enterprise, confidence is key. Confidence is more important than truthful math. Companies that enable confidence in their value selling processes will realize exceptional results.

The future of Value Management future is exciting, albeit, challenging. In a world where technology change is faster than the ability to adapt – how will you jumpstart your value journey?

The Value Management market is exploding; its trajectory and velocity are only going to accelerate. A mere 10 years ago, there were no Chief Digital Officers or Chief Customer Officers. Today, these roles are staples in the business world. Ten years from now, perhaps less, there will be a new and essential C-level executive:

The Chief Value Officer

CVOs will be common and the demand for Value Professionals will be incredible. The future is startlingly bright for those dedicated to Customer Value and Value Management. Wherever you are on your value journey, I hope this book inspires you to lean in and embrace Customer Value even more. Aggressively. Maniacally. Without pause or reservation.

Because, as Joe Sexton said, "Customer Value has always mattered." For the winners in today's digital age, and with as-a-service business models, Customer Value will be the primary thing that matters. Your business depends on it.

So...how will **_you_** jumpstart **_your_** value journey?

Good **_value_** selling!

Jim Berryhill
CEO & Co-Founder
DecisionLink Corporation